Scottish-German Links, 1550-1850

Second Edition

Scottish-German Links, 1550–1850

Second Edition

by
David Dobson

CLEARFIELD

INTRODUCTION

Scottish links with Germany can be traced back to the medieval period, for example on 11 October 1297 Andrew Moray and William Wallace, as guardians of the Community of Scotland and leaders of the Army of the Kingdom of Scotland, wrote to the mayors and citizens of Lubeck and Hamburg thanking them for their assistance in resisting English domination and offering them safe access to Scottish ports. However trade between them was relatively small scale, the emphasis of Scots commerce being with Scandinavia, the Baltic countries and the Netherlands. Consequently the settlement of Scots merchants and their factors was minimal and limited to ports such as Hamburg, Bremen, and Lubeck. The majority of Scots who were found in the various German principalities during the early modern period arrived as soldiers of fortune, especially during the Thirty Years War. Students also were attracted by the educational opportunities available in Germany, Wurzburg and Ratisbon in particular attracted the sons of Catholic families. While the emphasis of this book is on Scots in Germany and neighbouring countries in central Europe, it also contains a number of Germans found in Scottish records.

Since the first edition of this work was published in 2007 many new references have been uncovered which have been included in this second edition.

> David Dobson
> Dundee, Scotland.
> 2011

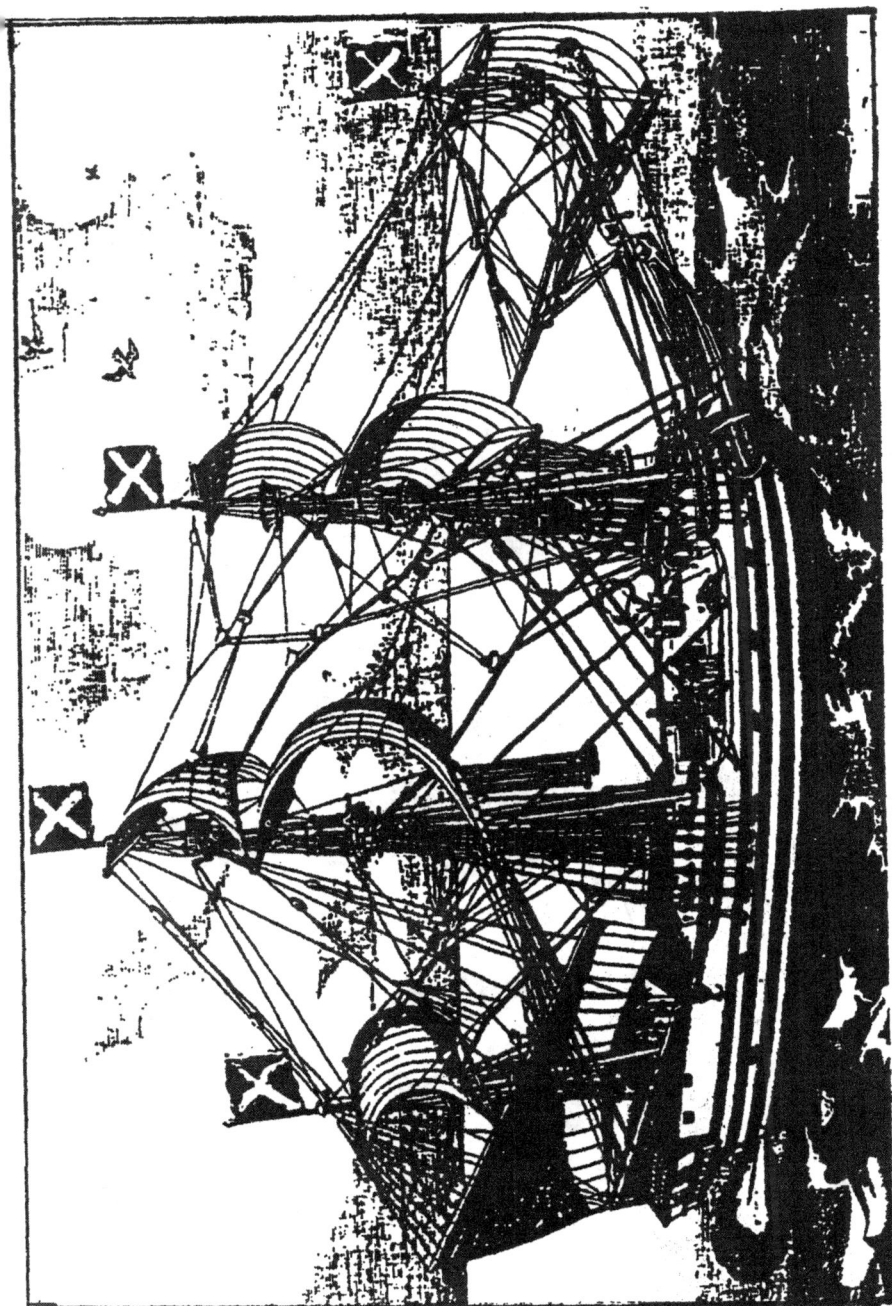

BREMEN

IN THE SIXTEENTH CENTURY

1

SCOTTISH-GERMAN LINKS, 1550-1850

ABENSUR, MOSES, a merchant in Hamburg, an inventory, 1873. [NRS.SC70.165/475]

ABERCROMBIE, ALEXANDER, son of Thomas Abercrombie of Gourdie, Angus, and his wife Grissel Sibbet, settled in Falkenburg, Duchy of Brandenburg, before 1606. Birth-brief issued 16 June 1606. [Dundee Burgh Archives]

ABERCROMBIE, JOHN CHRISTAIN, born 1641, professed at the Monastery of St James, Wurzburg, in 1669, a suspected priest who had returned to Scotland from Ratisbon or Windsburg, was imprisoned in Aberdeen Tolbooth in 1690, died in Scotland in 1714. [RPCS.XVI.469][SF#280]

ABERCROMBY, PATRICK, educated at the Braunsberg Seminary around 1596, died in 1611. [SIG#299]

ABERCROMBY, THOMAS, educated at the Braunsberg Seminary around 1599, later in Vilna. [SIG#299]

ABERCROMBY, WALTER, at the Ratisbon Seminary in 1713. [SIG#294][RSC#I.250]

ABERCROMBY, WILLIAM, educated at the Braunsberg Seminary around 1610. [SIG#299]

ABERCROMBIE, ..., from Aberdeen, a student in Germany before 1801, returned via Yarmouth and Dundee . [NRS.CE70.1.9/66]

ABERNETHY, ALEXANDER, at the Ratisbon Seminary in 1719, died in America. [SIG#294][RSC#I.251]

ABERNETHY, JOHN, at the Ratisbon Seminary in 1718. [SIG#294][RSC#I.250]

ADAM, ALEXANDER, in Stralsund, 5 May 1621. [Montrose Court Book]

ADAM, ROBERT, in Germany, 1756. [NRS.GD18/4812]

AIDIE, ANDREW, from Aberdeen, a student at the University of Heidelberg, matriculated on 4 May 1603, later Professor of Philosophy at Danzig. [SIG#314][SHR.V.67][RCPE]

AITKEN, JANE WALKER, daughter of Andrew Aitken in Edinburgh, married Samuel Pike from Reading, in Geneva on 28 April 1885. [S#13044]

ALEXANDER, ARCHIBALD, a student at the Scots College in Douai around 1648, went to Wurzburg in 1649. [SF#274]

ALEXANDER, CHARLES, from Edinburgh, at the Ratisbon Seminary in 1739. [SIG#294]

ALEXANDER, E., from the Diocese of Aberdeen, was admitted to the Monastery of Ratisbon on 18 September 1650. [SIG#292]

ALEXANDER, PATRICK JOHN, born 1658 in Aberdeen, ordained in Wurzburg in December 1679, died 25 May 1682. [AF#281]

AMINES, JOACHIM, skipper of the Stats Bremen, a bond, 1676. [NRS.RD4.39.658]

ANCRUM, Lady, to Hamburg and Emden in 1803. [NRS.GD40.7.93]

ANDERSON, ALEXANDER, from Aberdeen, a student at the University of Heidelberg, matriculated on 20 April 1603. [SIG#314][SHR.V.67][RCPE]

ANDERSON, ARCHIBALD, educated at the Braunsberg Seminary around 1587, became a Jesuit. [SIG#299]

ANDERSON, JOHN, of Teinet, matriculated at the Ratisbon Seminary in 1748. [SIG#295][RSC.I.252]

ANDERSON, JOHN B., a monk at the Scots Monastery at Wurzburg in 1791. [SIG#304]

ANDERSON, MARGARET, daughter of the late John Anderson of Gladswood, Berwickshire, married Captain G. Walter Story in Frankfort in 1835. [GA#5084]

ANDERSON, RICHARD, a student at the University of Helmstadt in 1603. [SIG#313]

ANDERSON, ..., a wright from Aberdeen, was recruited by Captain Hurrey to fight for the King of Bohemia, but deserted at Hamburg and returned to Aberdeen in 1620. [ACA.ACL.1.181]

ANDREW, NICOLAS and JANE, in Hamburg, 1657.

ANNES, JOACHIM, a skipper in Bremen, a bond re the purchase of the ship John of Culross in 1675. [NRS.GD29.1864]

ANNAN, ..., a Captain of the Swedish Army in Germany during the 1630s. [SIG#283]

ANSTRUTHER, ROBERT, diplomat in Hamburg, around 1630; in Frankfurt, 1633. [NRS.GD406.1.250/9305]

ANSTRUTHER, R., in Berlin,1795. [NRS.NRAS.3955.60.3.62]

APLER, GEORGE ADAM, a coachmaker from Wurtemburg, emigrated with his wife and three children from Rotterdam on the Hannah of Rotterdam, master William Wilson, bound via Leith to Philadelphia in 1746. Apler abandoned the voyage at Leith as his wife and children had died. [NRS.AC10.317/318]

ARBUTHNOTT, ALEXANDER, a student at the University of Rostock in 1584; a student at the University of Helmstadt in

1591, and a student at the University of Heidelberg in 1594, matriculated there on 30 July 1594. [SIG#313/314][SHR.V.67][RCPE]

ARBUTHNOTT, BENEDICT, born 5 March 1737, Abbot of the Monastery of St James at Ratisbon in 1776, died 19 April 1820. [St James gravestone]

ARBUTHNOTT, CHARLES, born 5 March 1737, at the Ratisbon Seminary in 1748. [SIG#295][RSC#I.252]

ARDUTHIE, HENRY, son of Thomas Arduthie and his wife Janet Merchant in Fetteresso, settled in Hamburg, died 1602. [MSC.II.41]

ARKLEMAN, CASPAR, a merchant in Hamburg, April 1684, 1692. [NRS.AC7.6; AC7.9]

ARMIN, ..., a Captain of the Swedish Army in Germany during the 1630s, wounded at Stralsund. [SIG#283]

ARMOUR, ALEXANDER, was a student at the Scots College in Douai around 1595, later a monk at Ratisbon. [SF#274]

ARNOTT, JAMES, educated at the Braunsberg Seminary around 1585, returned to Scotland. [SIG#299]

ARROT, WILLIAM, a Lieutenant Colonel, formerly in the service of the Elector of Brandenburg, 1689. [NRS.GD26.7.268]

ASHENHEIM, JACOB, was admitted as a burgess of Edinburgh on 9 January 1829. [EBR]

ASLOAN, GEORGE, a student at the Scots College in Douai around 1606, then at the Scots College in Rome in 1616, a monk who died in Germany. [SF#274/275]

ASLOAN, JOHN, born around 1595, of Garroch near Dumfries, matriculated at Wurzburg on 12 June 1625, Abbot of

Wurzburg from 1638 to 1661, possibly Abbot of Ratisbon from 1639 to 1646, died in January 1661. [SF#272, 279]

AUCHENLECK, HUGH, at the Ratisbon Seminary in 1719. [SIG#294][RSC#I.251]

AUCHENVOLE, THOMAS, born 1581 in Stirling, settled in Germany by 1614, died in 1653. [NRS.B66.25.50.1-4] [SIG#53]

BACKER, HANS PETER, master of the <u>Young Ary of Hamburg,</u> 1749. [NRS.AC11.74/75/76]

BACKHAUSEN, HANS, a merchant in Hamburg, a fishing co-partnership, 1669. [NRS.RD2.26.100]

BAILLIE, BERNARD, from Stirling, was admitted to the Monastery of Ratisbon on 2 February 1691, died 1743. [SIG#293]

BAILLIE, ALEXANDER, born 1590, of Carnbroe, was educated at the Scots College in Rome in 1612, then a monk at Wurzburg by 1617, administrator of Ratisbon from 1634 to 1636, Abbot of Erfurt from 1636 to 1646, Abbot of Ratisbon from 1646 to 1655, died near Ratisbon on 7 April 1655. [SF#275-279]

BAILLIE, GEORGE, of Jerviswood, a merchant in Hamburg, 1683. [NRS.RH15.49.7]

BAILLIE, WILLIAM, a Colonel of the Swedish Army in Germany during the 1630s. [SIG#283]

BAILLIE, WILLIAM, of Carphin, born 1633, was educated at the Scots College in Rome, from 1657 to 1658, then a monk in Wurzburg from 1658, died before June 1689 possibly in Britain. [SF#275-280]

BAIRD, JAMES OLIVER, born 26 March 1853, son of Reverend John Baird and his wife Elizabeth Hughes, died in

Hanover, Germany, on 25 January 1872. [F.2.96]

BAIRNSON, ..., master of the St Peter of Lubeck, May 1628.
[NRS.AC7.1]

BAKER, HANS PETER, master of the dogger Young Ary of
Hamburg, 1734. [NRS.AC11.74/75/76]

BAKER, PATRICK or PETER, a merchant in Holstein, bonds,
1666, 1670. [NRS.RD2.16.276; RD4.27.591]

BALFOUR, Captain DAVID, a soldier who served under
General Leslie in Germany, died before 1636.
[StAU:MS36220.682; HL#682]

BALFOUR, JAMES, a student at the University of Wittenberg,
1544. [SIG#305]

BALFOUR, JOHN, son of Patrick Balfour in the Canongate, a
prisoner in Canongate Tolbooth, was released to go as a
soldier under Colonel Sinclair to fight in Germany, in June
1628. [RPCS.II.333]

BALLANTINE, W., a Colonel of the Swedish Army in Germany
during the 1630s. [SIG#283]

BALLANTINE, WILLIAMINA, youngest daughter of the late
Alexander Ballantine in Edinburgh, married Richard Norton
Wright, at the British Embassy in Dresden on 3 January
1857. [W.XVIII.1834]

BANKS, WILLIAM, a merchant in Hamburg, 1750.
[NRS.AC8.731]

BANNERMAN, WILLIAM, son of William Bannerman and his
wife Katherine Ronaldson in Bogforlay, Aberdeenshire, a
burgess of Harisburg, Germany, in 1597. [APB]

BARCLAY, ALEXANDER, a banker in Hamburg, 1857.
[NRS.GD1.1220.49]

BARCLAY, DAVID, in Hamburg, 14 September 1590, wrote to the Chancellor and Council of Denmark. [DAC]

BARCLAY, DAVID, a merchant in Hamburg, 1717. [SIL#44]

BARCLAY, GEORGE, [Georg Barcklay], a merchant and 'civis primarius' in Anklam, near Griefswald, married Emerentia Rowan before December 1607 in Anklam, died there in 1615. [HKA]

BARCLAY, JAMES, born in 1617, son of Reverend James Barclay and his wife Bessie Duncan in Drumbled, Aberdeenshire, settled in Memel, Prussia, by 1635, a birth brief was issued by the magistrates of Aberdeen in 1661. [APB]

BARCLAY, JOHN, a merchant and citizen of Rostock, Mecklenburg, was issued by a birth brief by the magistrates of Banff on 29 March 1621; 1629. [NRS.RH1.2.874; RH16.209]

BARCLAY, PETER, a merchant and citizen of Rostock, Mecklenburg, was issued by a birth brief by the magistrates of Banff on 29 March 1621; 1629. [NRS.RH1.2.874; RH16.209]

BARCLAY, ROBERT, son of Walter Barclay of Mondurno and his wife Margaret Leslie, in Hungary by 1592. [MSC.II.17]

BARCLAY, ROBERT, a merchant from Shetland, in Hamburg, 1717, 1720, 1728, 1739. [NRS.RH15.93.17.20/21; AC8.379, 585][SIL#75/139]

BARCLAY, Sir ROBERT, married Madame de Cronstadt, daughter of Colonel Durell and the young widow of the late Baron de Cronstadt, in Hamburg on 20 June 1802. [Greenock Advertiser, #1/54]

BARCLAY, WILLIAM, born in 1626, son of Reverend James Barclay and his wife Bessie Duncan in Drumbled,

Aberdeenshire, settled in Dutchylle, Prussia, by 1643, a birth brief was issued by the magistrates of Aberdeen in 1661. [APB]

BARDEWISCH, HERMAN, a merchant in Bremen, a deed, 1702, [NRS.RD2.86.1.430]; then in Leith, 1722. [NRS.AC9.819]; in Kinghorn, Fife, 1723, master of the Patience of Bremen, 1723. [NRS.RH15.93.18/12/13]

BARKHOUSIN, HANS, a merchant in Hamburg, a contract of co-partnership, 1670. [NRS.RD4.26.756]

BARKLEY, BEREND, jr., a merchant in Bremen, was admitted as a burgess and guilds-brother of Glasgow on 17 May 1716. [GBR]

BARR, FIDELE, sometime of 28 Greenside Street, Edinburgh, died at Friedenwieler in the Duchy of Baden, inventory 2 March 1859 with the Commissariat of Edinburgh. [NRS]

BARRY, JAMES, in Hamburg, an inventory, 1871. [NRS.SC70.154/907]

BAUMGARTNER, JOHN, from England, a medical graduate of Edinburgh University, 1799. [EMG#30]

BAYLIE, HANNAH, married Jacob Coutons in the English Church of Hamburg on 28 September 1663. [TKH]

BAYLIES, Dr W., in Berlin, 1775. [NRS.NRAS.726.12.53]

BAYNE, PETER, editor of The Witness, married Clotilda Gerwien, eldest daughter of the late Major General Gerwein commander of a brigade in Prussian service, in Munster by the Reverend Shikedauz a minister of the Evangelical Church of Prussia on 26 April 1858. [W.XIX.1970]

BEATON, DAVID, was educated at the Braunsberg Seminary around 1596. [SIG#299]

BEATON, PAUL, Governor of Stettin, 1632. [MGIF.Map 3]

BEATON, ..., a Captain of the Swedish Army in Germany during the 1630s, wounded at Stralsund. [SIG#283]

BECCLAR, ..., a merchant in Hamburg, 1692. [NRS.AC7.9]

BECK, PETER, master of the St Andrew of Lubeck, 1670. [NRS.RH9.5.23]

BENJAMIN, BENJAMIN SIMON, born 1787 in Hamburg, a merchant, landed at Leith on 19 August 1818, residing at 94 Nicholson Street, Edinburgh, by 21 August 1818. [ECA.SL115.2.2/83]

BENNET, ALEXANDER, born in Patonlaws of Blairs, Kincardineshire, on 25 July 1839, was at the Ratisbon Seminary in 1852, ordained as a priest in 1862 and returned to Scotland on a mission, died in Perth on 25 March 1865. [SIG#296][RSC#I.258]

BENNET, JAMES, born 25 January 1818, was at the Ratisbon Seminary in 1830, died 29 September 1839. [SIG#295][RSC#I.255]

BERANDS, LUITIE, master of the Drie Gebroeders of Emden, 1731. [NRS.AC10.189]

BEREND, M., born in Altona, Lower Saxony, during 1778, later in Hamburg, a teacher of natural philosophy, arrived at Gravesend around 1802, resident of Glasgow and Edinburgh around 1812. [ECA.SL115.2.2/69]

BEST, JESSIE W., wife of Baron Carl Von Podewils in Bavaria, heir to her mother Ann Roger, wife of John Best in Liverpool, who died on 9 September 1852, 8 May 1876. [NRS.S/H]

BEYK, JOHN, a merchant in Hamburg, 1676. [NRS.AC7.4]

BIBERAUER, WILHELM THEODOR, only son of Reverend Michael Biberauer, married Christian Erskine Stuart, third daughter of J. A. Stuart, and grand-daughter of the late Charles Stuart of Dunairn, MD, at the Protestant Church in Graz on 14 February 1857. [W.XVIII.1845]

BILLERWELL, JANE, daughter of Reverend William Billerwell in Dysart, Fife, died in Hamburg on 9 March 1852. [FH]

BINNERETT, JACOB, [alias James Burrett], a merchant from Aachen who settled in Edinburgh, traded from Leith to Guinea before 1638, a member of the Scottish Guinea Company. [SHR]

BLACKHALL, WILLIAM, in the University of 'Bromyberrie', Prussia, son of Robert Blackhall, a burgess of Aberdeen, and his wife Elspeth Shand, a birth brief issued 1647. [APB]

BLAIR or HEPBURN, JAMES, professed at the Monastery of St James, Wurzburg around 1667, died at Monte Cassino on 1 October 1702. [SF#280]

BLUDWORTH, BARTHOLEMEW, a merchant in Hamburg, trading with Inverness, 1715. [NRS.GD23.6.33]

BOCK, JOSEPH MARIA, a teacher of languages in Falkirk, Stirlingshire, 1853. [NRS.NRAS.3250/45]

BODE, ..., daughter of Captain L. W. Bode, was born in Emmerberg, Hanover, on 19 September 1861. [W.XXII.2344]

BOG, ALEXANDER, a student at the Scots College in Douai around 1581, later a soldier or monk in Germany in 1598. [SF#274]

BOGILL, JAMES, in Hamburg, 1680. [NRS.RH15.106.387.6]

BOGILL, WILLIAM, in Hamburg, 1678. [NRS.RH15.106.305.6]

BONAR, WILLIAM, of Rossie, Fife, a Colonel in Swedish service who fought in Germany, later he settled in the Duchy of Bremen where he bought the Castle of Gnadenfeld, he died in 1674. Governor of Stettin, 1658. [SIG#283][MGIF.Map 3][NRS.NRAS#2838/bundle 424]

BOOTH, JAMES, a Scottish nurseryman, died in Flotbec near Hamburg on 28 December 1814. [SM#77.237]

BOOTH, JAMES GODFREY, a merchant in Hamburg, an inventory, 1871. [NRS.SC70.154/675]

BORDEWISCH, HERMAN, master of the Patience of Bremen in Kinghorn, Fife, letters, 1723. [NRS.RH15.93.18.13/14]

BORMAN, ESTIEN, master of the Esperance of Hamburg, 1627. [NRS.AC7.1.54]

BOSANQUET, JACOB, from Hamburg, was admitted as a burgess and guilds-brother of Edinburgh on 19 September 1744. [EBR]

BOSWELL, JAMES, in Leipzig, 1764. [NRS.NRAS#1368/bundle 22]

BOTTINGER, HEINRICH WILHELM, in Bavaria, an inventory, 1874. [NRS.SC70.169/1152]

BOUE, AMICUS, from Hamburg, a medical graduate of Edinburgh University in 1817. [EMG#53]

BOUE, C., born 1797 in Hamburg, a merchant, landed in Leith on 26 June 1817, residing at St Patrick's Square, Edinburgh, by July 1817. [ECA.SL115.2.2/79]

BOWMAN, WALTER, of Logie, a tutor in Germany, 1730s. [NRS.NRAS.494.bundle 19]

BOYTOUN, FRANCIS, a merchant in Hamburg, 1664, 1670. [NRS.RD2.26.100; RD4.26.756]

BRECHIN, ALEXANDER, son of David Brechin and his wife Elizabeth Duncan in Monifieth, Angus, a traveller in Lumberg, Duchy of Pomerania, Dundee birth brief dated 13 August 1633. [Dundee Burgh Archives]

BREUSCH, PETER, an engineer, paper maker at Canonmills, later at Restalrig, printer at Holyrood to King James VII, a Catholic.[OEC.XXV.54]

BROCKIE, MAR., from Edinburgh, was admitted to the Monastery of Ratisbon on 25 February 1708, died 1739. [SIG#293]

BRODIE, JOSEPH, born 20 August 1783, son of Reverend Alexander Brodie, minister of Carnbee, Fife, and his wife Helen Pitcairn, a merchant in Hamburg, died 14 March 1826. [F.V.190]

BROUGHTON, CHARLES, married Mary Wolfenden in the English Church of Hamburg on 7 May 1691. [TKH]

BROUNFIELD, WILLIAM, sergeant major under Colonel Sir John Ruthven serving in Germany, testament confirmed with the Commissariat of Edinburgh on 28 June 1637. [NRS]

BROWN, ALEXANDER, born 1639, professed in the Monastery of St James,Wurzburg, on 1 November 1660, died in England during September 1697. [SF#280]

BROWN, ANDREW, brother of Robert Brown, a merchant in Posa, Germany, 1661. [NRS.RD3.3.86]

BROWN, ANDREW, son of William Brown and his wife Marion Anderson in the Mill of Rubray, Forglen, Banffshire, a traveller in Germany, 1599. [APB]

BROWN, JAMES, professed in the Monastery of St James in Wurtzburg after 1632, died in March 1658. [SF#279]

BROWN, or **CONSTABLE, JAMES,** from East Fortune, was admitted to the Monastery of Ratisbon on 1 May 1698, died 1720. [SIG#293]

BROWN, JAMES, in Heligoland, 18 May 1847. [NRS.RD5.1026.241]

BROWN, JOHN, son of James Brown and his wife Margaret Shearer in Affleck, Kinnoir, settled in Kreustbrig, Hungary, before 1597. [APB]

BROWN, JOHN, a servant to Colonel Robert Douglas, at Lutze, 1638. [STAUL.HL#685]

BROWN, JOHN, a student at the Scots College in Douai around 1668, to Wurzburg in 1674. [SF#274]

BROWN, JOHN, eldest son of George Brown, 131 Clarence Place, Glasgow, died in Giessen, Germany, on 7 May 1849. [SG#1829]

BRUCE, ALEXANDER, of the Faculty of Law, Wurzburg University, Wurzburg, Bavaria, before 1603. [SNQ.IX.3rd.87]

BRUCE, ALEXANDER, [born 1629, died 1680], letters from Bremen. [NRS.NRAS.4235]

BRUCE, GEORGE AUGUSTINE, born near Edinburgh in 1659, to Wurzburg in October 1677, ordained in 1683, administrator in 1703-1613, abbot1713-1716, died 1716. [SF#280]

BRUCE, GEORGE C., married Auguste Caroline Hudtwalcker, third daughter of Herr Hudtwalcker, a senator of Hamburg, there on 20 May 1857. [W.XVIII.1874]

BRUCE, Sir HENRY, was appointed by Cardinal Francis Dietrichstein as commander of Nicolsburg (Mikoluv) on the frontier of Lower Austria 1619. [STW#110]

BRUCE, JAMES, from Clackmannan, was admitted to the Monastery of Ratisbon on 1 January 1682. [SIG#293]

BRUCE, STEPHEN, son of James Bruce and his wife Gilles Will, a traveller in Prussia, Dundee birth brief dated May 1612. [Dundee City Archives]

BRUCE, WILLIAM, Professor of Roman Law at the University of Wurzburg, Wurzburg, Bavaria, before 1593. [SNQ.IX.87]

BRUNTSFIELD, W., a Colonel of the Swedish Army in Germany during the 1630s, died at Buxtehude. [SIG#283]

BRYCE, ALEXANDER, in Trieste, Austria, was served heir to his father John Bryce there, who died on 26 December 1874. [NRS.S/H.5.3.1884]

BUCHANAN, JAMES, in Vienna, brother of Archibald Buchanan of Auchintirly, a letter, 1804. [NRS.GD1.512.34]

BUETTNER, ALEXANDER, MD, Berlin, applied to be admitted as a fellow of the Royal College of Physicians of Edinburgh in 1875. [NRS.NRAS#726/3/707]

BUHLEN, GEORG FREDERICH, a servant in Seagate, Dundee, 1769. [DCA.RS.15.286]

BURMEISTER, JOHN DERIK, factor for Joust Vansverberke, a merchant in Hamburg, a bond, 1682. [NRS.RD2.58.334]

BURNETT, ALEXANDER, British charge d'affaires in Berlin, 1746-1791. [NRS.NRAS.1368]

BURNETT, DUNCAN, from Aberdeen, a student at the University of Helmstadt in 1599. [SIG#313]

BURNETT, GEORGE, a cleric of the Diocese of Aberdeen, matriculated at the University of Koln in 1469. [SNQ.III.78]

BURNETT, GILBERT, from Mar, a student at the University of Helmstadt in 1591. [SIG#313]

BURROWS, JAMES, in Hamburg, was admitted as a burgess and guilds-brother of Ayr on 19 November 1756. [ABR]

BURTT, HENRY, Governor of Greifswald, 1643. [MGIF.Map 3]

BURTON, JAMES, a merchant in Hamburg, 1838. [NRS.B22.4.48/276]

BUTTERY, JOHN, educated at the Braunsberg Seminary around 1596, returned to Scotland. [SIG#299]

BYRES, ROBERT, a merchant in Memel, was admitted as a burgess of Montrose on 18 February 1767. [MBR]

CAESAR, JOHN JAMES, minister of the Reformed German Church in London, memorial, 1709-1712. [NRS.CH1.2.28.2/181-201]

CALLANDER, ..., daughter of Mrs Callander of Craigforth and Ardkinglas, was born at Schloss Ering, Bavaria, the seat of Count and Countess Paumgarten, on 18 December 1843. [W.V.423]

CAMERON, JOHN, from Glasgow, a student at the University of Heidelberg, 1607. [RCPE]

CAMERON, PATRICK, "Patritius Kymerina", a German-Scot, a student at the University of Heidelberg, matriculated on 12 June 1603. [SIG#314][SHR.V.67]

CAMERON, ROBERT, born 3 January 1823, was at the Ratisbon Seminary in 1838, returned to Scotland as a missionary, died in Falkirk on 10 January 1848. [SIG#295] [RSC#I.256]

CAMPBELL, COLIN, from Carwhin, in Munich and Vienna, letters, 1782. [NRS.GD112.39.1547/1548]

CAMPBELL, DAVID, late Lieutenant Colonel of the 9th Foot, died in Frankfurt on Maine on 3 July 1840. [GA#5622]

CAMPBELL, HENRIETTA, daughter of Robert Campbell in Stirling, died in Geneva on 16 February 1841. [W.II.120]

CAMPBELL, JAMES, s merchant in Hamburg, 1680. [NRS.RH15.106.387.6]

CAMPBELL, JEAN, wife of Richard Luke a merchant in Hamburg, 1746. [NRS.SC54.XIV, 25.9.1749] [NRS.GD65.194]; was served as heir to her aunt Ann Alexander, wife of Alexander Forbes a limner in Edinburgh, and to her mother Jean Alexander, wife of Archibald Campbell, Writer to the Signet, on 10 July 1754. [NRS.S/H]

CAMPBELL, JOHN ANDREW, (?), ["Johan Andreas Kambell"], a citizen of Hamburg, 1647. [St AH.Genealogische Sammlungen, 741-2, Register zum Burgerbuch, 1629-1663, 11 June 1647]

CAMPBELL, JOHN, born in Edinburgh, son of John Campbell of the Citadel and his wife Anne Caroline, died in Geneva on 11 August 1829. [Canongate gravestone]

CAMPBELL, JOHN ROBERT, versus Adelinde Holzbauer a flower maker in Munich, 1853. [NRS.NRAS.3250.43-44]

CAMPBELL OLYMPIA, second daughter of Sir Alexander Cockburn Campbell, and grand-daughter of Major General Sir John Malcolm, married Charles Uhde of Handschuheim, in Wiesbaden on 4 November 1857. [W.XVIII.1924]

CAMPBELL, W., Vice Consul of Stettin, second son of Dr John Campbell in Aberdeen, married Emily Cook, second daughter of the late C. J. Cook, JP in Essex, late of Madras, in the British Vice Consulate, Stettin, Prussia, on 15 August

1854. [W.XV.1576]

CAMPBELL, :...., daughter of J. Campbell of Treebanks, was born in Frankfort on Maine on 25 September 1843. [GA#5945]

CAMPBELL, ..., daughter of William Campbell, HM Consul in Stettin, was born in Eckerburg on 1 September 1855. [W.XVI.1689]

CAMPBELL, ..., daughter of James Campbell, was born in Stuttgart, Wurtemburg, on 19 March 1859. [S#71]

CARLIN, JOHN, born in Glasgow on 26 May 1838, was at the Ratisbon Seminary in 1852, later ordained as a priest, returned to Scotland, died on 29 August 1870. [SIG#296][RSC#I.258]

CARMICHAEL, GALLUS, Prior of the Scots Monastery at Wurzburg in 1785. [SIG#304]

CARMICHAEL, JAMES, was at Ratisbon Seminary in 1756. [SIG#295][RSC#I.253]

CARMICHAEL, JOHN, was at Ratisbon Seminary in 1756. [SIG#295][RSC#I.253]

CARMICHAEL, THOMAS, was at the Ratisbon Seminary in 1802. [SIG#295] [RSC#I.254]

CHALMERS, A., from Edinburgh, was admitted to the Monastery of Ratisbon on 15 April 1663, died in Italy. [SIG#292]

CHALMERS, DAVID, a student at the University of Rostock in 1592. [SIG#313]

CHALMERS, Sir JAMES, in Silesia, Germany, son of Gilbert Chalmers and his wife Christian Con in Kintore, Aberdeenshire, birth brief issued 1670. [APB]

CHALMERS, JESSIE LEWISA, born 1860, daughter of Lewis Chalmers, late of Fraserburgh, died in Eichstadt, Bavaria, in 1884. [DA#7279]

CHALMERS, JOHN, a student at the University of Heidelberg, matriculated on 2 December 1607. [SIG#314][SHR.V.67]

CHALMERS, M., from the Diocese of Aberdeen, admitted to the Monastery of Ratisbon on 13 November 1638. [SIG#292]

CHALMERS, THOMAS, educated at the Braunsberg Seminary around 1619, later in Rome and Scotland. [SIG#299]

CHAMBERS, GILBERT, was educated at the Scots College in Rome from 1635 to 1637, then a monk in Ratisbon. [SF#275]

CHAMBERS, WILLIAM, was educated at the Scots College in Rome in 1661, then a monk in Ratisbon. [SF#275]

CHAPMAN, ANDREW, son of John Chapman and his wife Elspet Forbes in Old Meldrum, Aberdeenshire, in Rossinburg, Prussia, 1590. [APB]

CHARLES, ALEXANDER, born 1730, son of a painter in Edinburgh, matriculated at the Ratisbon Seminary in 1739. [RSC#I.252]

CHEYNE, GREGORY, born around 1672, from Mar, matriculated at Wurzburg on 12 March 1695, ordained in 1697, died 1731. [SF#272, 281]

CHISHOLM, ALAN, born in Tweeddale about 1638, a novice in 1662, professed in the Monastery of St James, Wurzburg in 1663, matriculated at Wurzburg on 6 November 1694, died 1703. [SF#272, 280]

CHISHOLM, ["SYSHOLMS"], THOMAS, a Scots glovemaker, married J. Elis from Altona, in St Pauli, Hamburg, 1696. [TKH.82]

CHRYSTIE, ROBERT, a traveller in Lauenburg, Pommern, son of James Chrystie in Adamstown, Angus, and his wife Agnes Scugell, Dundee birth brief dated 22 August 1607. [Dundee City Archives]

CLARK, PETER and KATHERINE, (?), in Hamburg, 1620

CLOCH, BROCHART, a citizen of Lubeck, 1545. [NRS.GD149.264.F210]

CLOKNER, LEWIS, born 1833 in Germany, a street musician in Edinburgh by 1851. [Census]

CLUNEO, WARMEVOLT, master of the Nightingale of Hamburg, 1627. [NRS.AC7.1.2]

CLYNE, JAMES, a leather merchant from Aberdeen, died in Oberwerth near Coblentz on 2 July 1866. [DA#1625]

COCHRANE, Sir JOHN, a military officer in Hamburg, 1640s. [SSNE#1490]

COGHILL-CAMPBELL-SIMSON, JOHN, and his wife Mary Von Reifeld, 1866. [NRS.NRAS.3250/66]

COINDET, JOHN CHARLES, from Geneva, graduated MD at Edinburgh University in 1820. [EMG#61]

COLINSON, F., from Aberdeen, was admitted to the Monastery of Ratisbon on 2 February 1667, died 1686. [SIG#293]

COLINSON, GEORGE, was educated at the Scots College in Rome from 1661 to 1665, later became a Benedictine in Ratisbon. [SF#275]

COLINSON, Captain ROBERT, servant of the Earl of Wintoun, trading with Danzig, Lubeck and Bremen, accounts, 1684-1689. [NRS.RH9.1.176]

COLT, OLIVER, a student at the University of Heidelberg, 1570.

[SIG#314][SHR.V.67]

COLMUS, HARRY, a merchant in Hamburg, a contract of co-partnership, 1670. [NRS.RD4.26.756]

CONNAGHAN, JOSEPH, born in Glasgow on 5 May 1835, was at the Ratisbon Seminary in 1852, ordained as a priest, died in Glasgow on 18 January1877. [SIG#296][ESC#I.258]

CONWAY, JANE MARY, daughter of the late Henry Conway in Edinburgh, and wife of Lieutenant Siegmund Sixt Von Armin, AD, died in Cologne on 20 February 1879. [S#11,115]

COOKE, ANDREW, from the Diocese of Aberdeen, was admitted to the Monastery of Ratisbon on 18 October 1671, died 1721. [SIG#293]

COOKE, JOHN AMBROSE, born in Preston around 1660, matriculated at Wurzburg on 9 August 1690, Abbot from 1689 to 1703, died in Dusselthal in 1727. [SF#281]. [SF#272]

COOPER, JOSHUA, (?), in Hamburg, 1622.

CORDES, PETER, of Hamburg, was admitted as an honorary burgess and guilds-brother of Glasgow on 15 November 1779. [Glasgow Burgess Roll]

COSTER, CLAUS, a merchant in Hamburg, bonds, 1677, 1680. [NRS.RD4.40.599; RD4.47.322]

COWAN, Mrs JANE, born 1809, wife of Alexander Cowan, Writer to the Signet, died in Bonn on 8 January 1831. [GA#3624]

COSTER, KATHERINE, widow of Claus Coster a merchant in Hamburg, a bond, 1683. [NRS.RD3.55.183]

CRAIG, JAMES, born 1835, late Inspector of the Poor of St

Cuthbert's Combination, died in Davos Platz, Switzerland, on 17 October 1884. [S#12879]

CRAIG, JOHN, son of Robert Craig, burgess of Edinburgh, and his wife Katherine Bellenden, a graduate of St Andrews then a student in Germany, birth brief dated 29 July 1574. [ECA.Moses/270/8459]

CRAIG, JOHN, a student at the University of Helmstadt in 1605. [SIG#313]

CRAIG, JOHN, from the Lothians, settled in Greifswald, Germany, by 1628. [NRS.RS24.13.267]

CRANACH, DAVID, brother of John Cranach the Bishop of Brechin, a priest of the Diocese of Aberdeen, matriculated at the University of Koln in 1442. [SNQ.3/X.77]

CRANSTON, ROBERT, fought in Germany and Poland, returned to Scotland, Bishop of Dunkeld, died in May 1685. [Meigle MI]

CRANSTOUN, Captain, at battle of Hogstadt, 1704. [NRS.GD44.14.4.6]

CRAWFORD, JAMES, in Hamburg, a letter, 1798. [NRS.NRAS#3955/60/1/44]

CRAWFORD, JOHN, son of ...... Crawford, a butcher, a prisoner in Edinburgh tollbooth, was released to go as a soldier under Colonel Sinclair to fight in Germany, in June 1628. [RPCS.II.333]

CRAWFORD, JOHN ARCHIBALD, in Dresden, 1862. [NRS.RD5.1358.173]

CRAWFORD, ROBERT, in Magdeburg, letters, 1795-1800. [NRS.GD216.237.1/2; GD216.238]

CRICHTON, D., in Hanover, 1751. [NRS.NRAS#234/box

47/4/84]

CRICHTON, PLACID, of Auchengoul, professed on the Monastery of Wurzburg in 1689, died 1730. [SF#281]

CRIGHTON, GEORGE, at the Ratisbon Seminary in 1719. [SIG#294]

CRIGHTON, GEORGE, born 25 September 1725, matriculated at the Ratisbon Seminary in 1735. [RSC#I.251]

CRIGHTON, GREGOR, of Auchingowell, Diocese of Aberdeen, was admitted to the Monastery of Ratisbon on 25 March 1684, died 1748. [SIG#293]

CRIGHTON, WILLIAM, eldest son of Sir A. W. Crighton, MD, died in Manheim on 23 November 1837. [DPCA#1846]

CRUDEN, WILLIAM, of Gategill, died in Hanau, Germany, 24 April 1838, inventory, 1838, Comm. Edinburgh. [NRS]

CRUICKSHANK, ALEXANDER, son of Patrick Cruickshank a merchant in Aberdeen, a servant in Hungary around 1729. [ACA.APB.2.183]

CRUICKSHANKS, JAMES, was at the Ratisbon Seminary in 1800. [SIG#295]

CRUICKSHANK, JOHN, MD, at the Ratisbon Seminary in 1713. [SIG#294][RSC#I.249]

CRUIKSHANK, JAMES, son of John Cruikshank and his wife Agnes Garwick in Kincousie, a traveller in Holstein, 1593. [APB]

CRUKSHANK, WILLIAM, son of Andrew Crukshank and his wife Beigge Lesly in Meikle Durno, settled in Wersoy, Prussia, by 1589. [APB]

CUMMING, BEROALD, son of Andrew Cumming in Tuchill,

23

parish of Deer, Aberdeenshire, a merchant traveller in Prussia who died in December 1588. [APB]

CUMMING, THOMAS, Scots-Flemish, a student at the University of Heidelberg, matriculated on 28 May 1614. [SIG#314][SHR.V.67][RCPE]

CUNNINGHAM, ADAM, son of Adam Cunningham, a Lieutenant in the German Army, issued with a birth brief, stating his links to the family of William Cunningham, Earl of Glencairn, prior to his departure for Germany on 4 September 1662. [RGS.XI.318]

CUNNINGHAM, ALEXANDER, Governor of Heiligenstadt, 1634. [MGIF.Map 3]

CUNNINGHAM, ROBERT, Governor of Demmion, 1636. [MGIF.Map 3]

CUNNINGHAM, ROBERT, a student at the University of Greifswald in 1649. [SIG#314]

DALHUSIUS, JAN HERMAN, a former inspector in 'Weedin', a religious refugee who was persecuted by the Abbot of Romensdorf and escaped via Westphalia, Copenhagen, and England to Scotland in 1691. [RPCS.XVI.20]

DANIEL, MOSES, born 1741 in the city of Hanover, a spectacle-maker in Holland, moved via Gravesend to England in 1775, later settled in Canongate, Edinburgh, in 1786. [ECA.SL115.2.1/86]

D'ASTI, ALEXANDER, born in Germany, moved to London in 1760, married in Liverpool in 1764, settled in Scotland in 1772, father of 24 children, a teacher of modern languages, music and fencing, resident of the Grassmarket, Edinburgh, in 1794. [ECA.Aliens Register]

DATIWEILL, ..., a Lieutenant of Brigadier Slirler's Regiment of Swiss, was admitted as a burgess and guildsbrother of

Glasgow on 26 June 1719. [GBR]

DAVIDSON, ANDREW, a messenger in Moffat, was found guilty of adultery but was allowed to enlist under Alexander, Lord Spynie, instead of being punished, in 1627, however he absconded and returned to Annandale. Subsequently he was summoned to appear before the Privy Council to explain his actions [RPCS.II.183/562]

DAVIDSON, GEORGE, born in Letterfurie, near Buckie, Banffshire, on 19 November 1845, was at the Ratisbon Seminary in 1852, was ordained as a priest and returned to Scotland where he died on 6 July 1865. [SIG#296][RSC#I.258]

DAVIDSON, JAMES, born 20 September 1833 in Poutingbrae, Buckie, Banffshire, was at the Ratisbon Seminary from 1845 to 1848. [SIG#296][RSC#I.257]

DAVIDSON, WILLIAM, a merchant from Dundee, in Hamburg, 1665. [SSNE#5382]

DAYRS, PATRICK, a student at Frankfurt-on-the-Oder in 1576. [SIG#313]

DAWSON, JOHN, from Dalkeith, was naturalised in the Kingdom of Hungary by Leopold, Emperor of Germany, on 13 February 1661. [NRS.GD103/2/175]

DEASON, JOHN, born 1 February 1774 in Huntly, Aberdeenshire, matriculated at the Ratisbon Seminary in 1788, ordained as a priest on 11 March 1797, died 21 November 1855. [RSC#I.254]

DE BARRY, DAVID, partner of the Nightingale of Bremen, deeds, 1673. [NRS.RD3.33.721/724]

DE CARRO, JOHN, from Geneva, a medical graduate of Edinburgh University, 1793. [EMG#24]

DE KEPPELL, Baron WILLIAM, a.d.c.to General Keple of the

Swiss Regiment, was admitted as a burgess and guildsbrother of Glasgow on 29 July 1719. [GBR]

DENHAM, THOMAS, born in Edinburgh on 11 November 1725 son of Sir Archibald Denham and his wife Jane Warrender, died in Ashfeldt, Hess, on 22 March 1761. [Greyfriars gravestone, Edinburgh]

DE LARRY, HARRY, Captain of the Prince Royal Regiment of Prussia, was admitted as a burgess and guilds-brother of Glasgow on 29 July 1719.[GBR]

DENNISTOUN, ANNE PENELOPE CAMPBELL, daughter of James Robert Dennistoun, married John Guthrie Smith, from Glasgow, fourth son of William Smith of Carbeth-Guthrie, in the British Embassy, Stuttgart, on 26 January 1861. [W.XXII.2272]

DE VIVRE, FREDERICK, born 1816 in Switzerland, a butler in Edinburgh by 1851. [Census]

DEVLIN, AHREND GEEHDEN, born 1790 in Groote Veen, Hanover, master of the galliot Aurora, buried in Dundee on 15 September 1838. [Dundee Burial Register]

DEWAR, WILLIAM, in Baden Baden, heir to his grandmother Jane Allison who died on 20 May 1860, widow of John James Gaugain a merchant in Edinburgh, 13 August 1868. [NRS.S/H]

DE WELDEREN, Baron BERNARD, was admitted as a burgess and guildsbrother of Glasgow on 29 July 1719. [GBR]

DEY, MARTIN, a sailor on the King David of Hamburg, 27 January 1683. [NRS.RD3.55.183]

DEYENCE, LAMBERT, born in Germany during 1855, a resident of the City Poorhouse, Glasgow, in 1881. [1881 Census]

DEYER, JURGEN, master of the Fortune of Lubeck, 21 July 1628. [NRS.AC7.1.164]

DIAMOND, MARK, born 2 November 1817, matriculated at the Ratisbon Seminary in 1830, died 23 September 1839. [RSC#I.255]

DICKSON, ALEXANDER, born 1781 son of Peter Dickson, a farmer, and his wife Ann Dewar, formerly an engineer in Berlin, died in Wheatlands, Kirkliston, West Lothian, on 6 January 1824. [Kirkl;iston gravestone]

DICKSON, ANDREW, a priest of the Diocese of Aberdeen, matriculated at the University of Koln in 1480. [SNQ.X.3/78]

DIEDERICH, JOHANN, burgomaster of Hamburg, a merchant in Whalsay, Shetland Islands, a bond, 1683. [NRS.RD3.55.184]

DINGWALL, JAMES, born 1776, son of John Dingwall of Ralneston, Aberdeenshire, died in Hamburg on 12 January 1848. [EEC#21621]

DITKIN, HELINK, master of the Nightingale of Bremen, deeds, 1673. [NRS.RD3.33.721/724/726/727]

DIXON, MAURUS, born 1618, matriculated at Wurzburg on 27 November 1641, studied logic, ordained in 1645, Abbot from 1661 to 1679, died 16 March 1679. [SF#272, 280]

DOCHERTY, SAMUEL, born in Glasgow on 6 June 1838, was at the Ratisbon Seminary in 1852, and by 1862 he was in Dublin studying theology, died in San Francisco. [SIG#296] [RSC#I.258]

DON, GEORGE, in Bremen, 1797. [NRS.NRAS#3955/60/1/29]

DONALDSON, ANDREW, from the Diocese of Aberdeen, matriculated at the University of Koln in 1480.

[SNQ.X.3/78]

DONALDSON, JAMES URE, of Auchairne, Ayrshire, died in Passau, Bavaria, on 5 April 1885. [S#13025]

DONALDSON, JOHN, a traveller in Prussia, son of Arthur Donaldson and his wife Christian Ferrier, Dundee birth brief dated 21 May 1610. [Dundee Burgh Archives]

DONALDSON, ROBERT, a traveller in Germany, son of John Donaldson a burgess of Dundee and his wife Bessie Ireland, Dundee birth brief dated 26 June 1606. [Dundee Burgh Archives]

DONALDSON, [Donatzen], THOMAS, a small trader in Wismar, 1571. [SIG#50]

DONALDSON, WALTER, from Aberdeen, a student at the University of Heidelberg, matriculated on 11 September 1599. [SIG#314][SHR.V.67][RCPE]

DONALDSON, [Donatzen], WILLIAM, a small trader in Wismar, 1571. [SIG#50]

DOUGLAS, BERNARD, professed in the Monastery of Wurzburg by 1697, died in Bohemia in 1703. [SF#281]

DOUGLAS, Sir GEORGE, a Major General of the Swedish Army in Germany during the 1630s; Governor of Kreuznach, 1632-1635; died in Hamburg, 1636. [NA.SP75/13.f.323] [MGIF.Map. 3][SIG#283]

DOUGLAS, GEORGE LEWIS AUGUSTUS, youngest son of John Douglas, died in Thuringen, Voralberg, Austria, on 15 September 1854. [W.XV.1584]

DOUGLAS, GEORGE SHOLTO, 16th Earl of Morton, married Frances Theodore Rose in Berlin, 1817. [NRS.GD150.2274]

DOUGLAS, JAMES, in Stanhouend, Germany, 1625. [NRS.RS24.10.225]

DOUGLAS, Captain JAMES, in Stanehaven, Germany, 1642. [NRS.GD29.999]

DOUGLAS, JOHN, 53rd Foot, Guderarde, probate 20 December 1805. [NA.Prob.11/1434]

DOUGLAS, JOHN, in Hamburg, heir to his father John Sharp Douglas a merchant here who died on 15 April 1847, re a property in Argyle Street, Glasgow, 21 July 1866. [NRS.S/H]

DOUGLAS, NAOMI, 3rd daughter of the late Walter Douglas in Glasgow, married James Douglas, only son of James Douglas MD in Quebec, in Frankfort-on-Main, 15 November 1860. [GM.NS2/9.664]

DOUGLAS, ROBERT, a General of the Swedish Army in Germany, son of Patrick Douglas of Standingstone, Lothian, and his wife Christina Lessels, 1648. [RGS.IX.1995]; a bond dated Lutze, 1638; Governor of Schwaben, 1648-1650. [STW#285][MGIF.Map 3] [STAUL:HL#685][SIG#282]

DOUGLAS, WILLIAM, educated at the Braunsberg Seminary around 1596, later in Vilna. [SIG#299]

DOUGLAS, WILLIAM, educated at the Braunsberg Seminary around 1607, became a soldier. [SIG#299]

DOWNIE, Sir ALEXANDER, MA, in Giessen, physician to the British Embassy in Frankfurt, graduated MD at King's College, Aberdeen, on 2 April 1846. [KCA]

DRUMMOND, ['Duramenus'], DAVID, a student at the University of Heidelberg, 1597. [RCPE]

DRUMMOND, Sir DAVID, in Litniorits, Bohemia, 1634.

[NRS.GD406.1.9336]

DRUMMOND, CHARLES, of the family of the Duke of Perth, was at Ratisbon Seminary in 1756. [SIG#295][RSC#I.252]

DRUMMOND, Sir DAVID, a Major General in Swedish service in Germany, 1630s, [SIG#282]; Governor of Stettin, 1632. [MGIF.Map 3] in Litniorits, Bohemia, 1634. [NRS.GD406.1.9336]

DRUMMOND, DAVID, was at Ratisbon Seminary in 1772. [SIG#295][RSC#I.253]

DRUMMOND, Captain GEORGE, an army captain in Germany, 1760-62. [NRS.GD24.1.843]

DRUMMOND, JOHN, from Edinburgh, Ensign of a regiment in Swedish service which was shipped from Leith via Cromarty to Stralsund, Germany, in 1638. [RPCS.7.84]

DRUMMOND, JOHN, ADC to the King of Prussia around 1752. [EU.Laing Charters#3190]

DRUMMOND, MARY HOME, in Munich, a letter, 1845. [NRS.GD24.5.137]

DUFF, CHARLES, in Berlin, 1798. [NRS.NRAS#3955/60/3/1]

DUFF, THOMAS, born before 1594, from Maldavit near Culle, Banffshire, educated at the Braunsberg Seminary around 1610, later at the Monastery of Pelplin near Danzig. [SIG#299]; possibly also at the Scots College in Rome before becoming a Benedictine in Germany, matriculated at Wurzburg on 14 March 1629, a priest, died after 1636. [SF#272-275-279]

DUFF, THOMAS ABERCROMBY FRASER, born 1834, late of the 62nd Regiment, died in Bensheim near Darmstadt on 12 March 1857. [W.XVIII.1851]

DUGUID, JOHN, was at Ratisbon Seminary in 1764. [SIG#295][RSC#I.253]

DUGUID, ROBERT, was at the Ratisbon Seminary in 1723. [RSC#I.251]

DUMAN, ANN, third daughter of Jacob Duman sugar refiner, born in Hanover, Germany, and his wife Mary, daughter of Henry Bristow Hartshorn manufacturer in Ayliff Street, Whitechapel, London, born 6 August and baptised 25 August 1811 in Dundee. [St Paul's Episcopal Cathedral baptismal register]

DUMAN, CATHARINE, 4th daughter of Jacob Duman sugar refiner, born in Hanover, Germany, and his wife Mary, daughter of Henry Bristow Hartshorn manufacturer in Ayliff Street, Whitechapel, London, born 16 January, baptised 13 February 1814 in Dundee. [St Paul's Episcopal Cathedral Baptimal Register]

DUNBAR, E., from the Diocese of Argyll, was admitted to the Monastery of Ratisbon on 29 July 1674. [SIG#293]

DUNBAR, JAMES or JOHN, a captain in Bohemia, 1620. [STW#111]

DUNBAR, Major JAMES, Governor of Breitenburg, 1627. [MGIF.Map 3]

DUNBAR, JOHN, from the Diocese of Argyll, was admitted to the Monastery of Ratisbon on 1 March 1681. [SIG#293]

DUNBAR, NICOLAS, settled in the Monastery of Ratisbon in Bavaria, became a subject of the Duke of Bavaria, captured at Fedderate, imprisoned in the Canongate Tolbooth, Edinburgh, in 1691. [RPCS.XVI.529]

DUNCAN, AUGUSTUS, was admitted to the Monastery of Ratisbon on 8 September 1736. [SIG#294]

DUNCAN, JAMES, son of Duncan Duncan and his wife Anne

Simpson in Newburgh, Aberdeenshire, a traveller in Neumark, Brandenburg, died there in May 1590. [APB]

DUNCAN, JAMES, born 1834, was at the Ratisbon Seminary from 1845 to 1848. [SIG#296][RSC#I.257]

DUNCAN, JOHN, son of John Duncan, a mariner, and his wife Bessie Vauss, a traveller in Prussia around 1607. [Dundee City Archives, birth brief, 13 July 1607]

DUNCAN, ROBERT, a traveller in Pomare, [Pomerania], son of David Duncan in Fowlis, Angus, and his wife Katherine Lecky, birth brief dated 16 June 1606, Dundee. [Dundee Burgh Archives]

DUNMORE, THOMAS, in Hamburg, 1794, son of Robert Dunmore in Kelvinside, Glasgow. [NRS.GD1/850/50, 51; NRAS.NA20830]

DUNN, ALEXANDER, son of Peter Dunn and his wife Margaret Simson in Slioch, Drumblade, settled in Prussia during 1589. [APB]

DUNN, JAMES, a cleric of the Diocese of Aberdeen, graduated from the University of St Andrews in 1462, matriculated at the University of Koln in 1468. [SNQ.X.3/78]

DUNN, JOHN, son of James Dunn and his wife Margaret Mathewson in Parkhill, a traveller in Danzig and Prussia, 1589. [APB]

DUNN, JOHN, son of Thomas Dunn, a dyer burgess of Aberdeen, and his wife Margaret Davidson, in Anderburg, Germany, 1602. [APB]

DUNN, PATRICK, a student at the University of Helmstadt in 1603, and at the University of Heidelberg, matriculated on 9 May 1607. [SIG#313/314][SHR.V.67]

DUNN, ROLAND WILLIAM, born 1644, professed in the

Monastery of St James, Wurzburg on 1 November 1660, died in Northumberland on 20 August 1675. [SF#280]

DURHAM, DAVID, a student at the University of Heidelberg, matriculated on 27 January 1587. [SIG#314][SHR.V.67]

DURIE, JOHN, a theologian in Hamburg, 1634-1640. [CSPD. 1634.55; CSPD.1640.318][NRS.GD406.1.869]

DURNO, JAMES, in Berlin, a letter, 1792. [NRS.NRAS.3956.0.1.181]

DURRNER, JOHN, born 1812 in Bavaria, a music teacher in Edinburgh by 1851. [Census]

DURWARD, WILLIAM, a traveller in Butzow, Dukedom of Mecklenburg, son of Charles Durward and his wife Margaret Gray in Balneaves, Dundee, was granted a birth brief dated 9 September 1616. [Dundee Burgh Archives]

DUTHIE, HENRY, a burgess of Hamburg – see RPCS

DYSART, ALEXANDER, son of William Dysart, a burgess of Aberdeen, and his wife Janet Whyte, a traveller in Prussia, 1596. [APB]

EBELING, JOHN THEODORE PHILIP CHRISTIAN, "Zuneburgo-Germano", graduated MA, MD, from the University of Glasgow in 1779. [RGG]

EDMONSTONE, Captain THOMAS, in Berlingheim, 1744. [NRS.GD27/6/27]

EDWARD, JOHN, a student at Frankfurt-on-the Oder in 1589. [SIG#313]

ELLIOT, ELEANOR MARY, youngest daughter of James Elliot of Wolflee, married Baron de Poellnitz, at the house of the British Ambassador in Franfurt-on- Maine in 1841. [W.II.179]

ELPHINSTONE, WILLIAM, in Hamburg, in 1631.
[NRS.GD406.1.9305]

ERSKINE, ALEXANDER, born 31 October 1598, General in
Swedish service in Germany, married (2) Lucie Christine
von Malzahn, nee von Wartensleben, settled in Bremen,
died 24 August 1656. [Bremen Cathedral ms]

ERSKINE, Colonel THOMAS, a resident of Luneburg from
1686.

ERSKINE, WALTER, and his wife Anne Forest, settled in
Greifswald, Pomerania, parents of Alexander born there on
31 October 1598. [SIG#201]

ERSKINE, WALTER, in Grippiswald, trading with Dundee,
1614. [DSL]

ESTELL, ALEXANDER, son of George Estell and his wife
Katherine Steven at the Bridge of Don, Aberdeen, a burgess
of Wermer, Prussia, in 1601. [APB]

ESTER-HAZY, Prince NICOLAI, General of Artillery, Captain
of the Noble Hungarian Guard, Austrian Imperial
Ambassador, was admitted as a burgess of Glasgow on 29
August 1821. [GBR]

EWART, JOSEPH, in Berlin, 1791. [NRS.GD51.6.911]

EWART, ..., in Berlin, 1787. [NRS.NRAS#1054/bundle 130]

FAIRHOLME, GEORGE K. E., third son of the late George
Fairholme of Greenknowe, Berwickshire, married Pauline
Anelia Poellnitz, eldest daughter of Baron Frederic Poellnitz
of Chateau Frankenberg, Bavaria, at the British Embassy in
Frankfurt on 14 January 1857. [W.XVIII.1834]

FAIRHOLME, ..., daughter of George K. E. Fairholme of Old
Melrose, was born in Wurzburg, Bavaria, on 23 May 1861.
[W.XXII.2309]

FAIRHOLME, ..., son of George K. E. Fairholme, was born in Wurzburg, Bavaria, in 1862. [Hawick Advertiser]

FAIRLIE, Reverend JOHN, married Hannah Muldrop Fraser, only daughter of Thomas Aitken Fraser a merchant in Edinburgh, in Friedrichsdorf, Homburg, Germany, on 11 September 1873. [GH#10520]

FALCONER, COSMO, at the Ratisbon Seminary in 1719. [SIG#294]

FALCONER, COSMO, born on 9 November 1723, matriculated at the Ratisbon Seminary in 1735. [RSC#I.251]

FALCONER, JOSEPH, from Edinburgh, was admitted to the Monastery of Ratisbon on 1 January 1682, died 1732. [SIG#293]; matriculated at Wurzburg on 3 February 1695, studied theology. [SF#272]

FALLER, LUDWIG, born in Baden 1818, a clockmaker in Miller's Close, Murraygate, Dundee, buried 10 October 1852. [Dundee Burial Register]

FARQUHAR, AGNES, in Lausanne, Switzerland, inventory, 29 July 1859, with the Commissariat of Edinburgh. [NRS]

FARQUHARSON, ROBERT ALEXANDER, MD, in Berlin, Prussia, heir to his father Donald Farquharson postmaster in Ballater, Aberdeenshire, who died on 20 December 1852, 27 January 1868. [NRS.S/H]

FARQUHARSON, JOHN, born 1728, matriculated at the Ratisbon Seminary in 1739. [SIG#294][RSC#I.252]

FARQUHARSON, ROBERT ALEXANDER, a physician in Berlin, son of Donald Farquharson, the postmaster of Ballater, Aberdeenshire, who died on 20 December 1852. [NRS.S/H.1868]

FARQUHARSON, W., born in Monaltrie 1754, died in Vivars,

Switzerland, on 28 November 1828. [Tullich gravestone, Aberdeenshire]

FEHRS, JULIA, born 1828 in Holstein, a nursery maid in Edinburgh by 1851. [Census]

FERENBACH, PIUS, born 1809 in Baden, a master clockmaker in Edinburgh by 1851. [Census]

FERGUSON, KENNETH, Charge d'Affaires for Great Britain at the Court of Dresden, testament confirmed with the Commissariat of Edinburgh on 27 April 1789. [NRS]

FERGUSON, LUDOVIC, born in Edinburgh on 3 January 1815, a priest at the Ratisbon Seminary from 1841 to 1853. [RSC#I.256]

FERGUSON, PATRICK, in Germany, 1762. [NRS.GD32.24.62]

FERNUS, THOMAS, from the Diocese of Aberdeen, matriculated at the University of Koln in 1512. [SNQ.X.3/78]

FETTES, WILLIAM, born 1788 son of Sir William Fettes of Comelybank, Edinburgh, an advocate, died in Berlin on 13 June 1815. [Canongate gravestone]

FIDDES, (?), "FIDELIS", **JOHN,** a student and later Professsor at Frankfurt-on-the Oder, 1547. [SIG#313]

FINNE, CHRISTIAN LEWIS, chaplain to the King of Prussia and minister of the Reformed Church at Crossere, Silesia, formerly at Breslau, petition, 1759. [NRS.CH1/2/199/fo.180]

FINNY, MAC., from Buchan, was admitted to the Monastery of Ratisbon on 24 June 1694. [SIG#293]

FLEMING, HENRY, a Colonel of the Swedish Army in Germany during the 1630s. [SIG#283]

FLEMING, P., from Kirkoswald, Ayrshire, was admitted to the Monastery of Ratisbon on 21 November 1669, died 8 January 1720. [SIG#293]

FLETCHER, ALEXANDRINA, in Dresden, heir to her father Reverend Alexander Fletcher in London who died on 30 September 1860. [NRS.S/H]

FLUGGIR, LAURENTZ, in Hamburg, 1643. [NRS.GD83, Sec.2/195]

FOGO, GEORGE LAURIE, born 25 June 1847, son of John Laurie Fogo of Row, Perthshire, graduated MA from Glasgow University in 1867, minister of the Scots Church in Dresden from 1871, returned to Scotland in 1883, died 1 December 1912. [F.2.301]

FORBES, ALEXANDER, a student at the University of Heidelberg, matriculated on 11 June 1603. [SIG#314][SHR.V.67][RCPE]

FORBES, ALEXANDER, later tenth Lord Forbes, a Lieutenant General of the Swedish Army in Germany, [SIG#282]

FORBES, CHARLOTTE, born 1774, died in Lausanne, Switzerland, on 22 November 1856. [W.XVII.1820]

FORBES, GEORGE, a student at the University of Helmstadt in 1606, later Professor of Theology there. [SIG#313]

FORBES, JOHN, a student at the University of Heidelberg, 1613. [RCPE]

FORBES, Lord JAMES OCHENCAR, died in Breginz, Germany, inventory, 4 May 1843, with the Commissariat of Edinburgh. [NRS]

FORBES, JOHN, a student at the University of Heidelberg, matriculated on 8 October 1613. [SIG#314][SHR.V.67]

FORBES, JOHN, Captain under Major Robert Hog, who died in the Emperor's Service, son of Thomas Forbes, a baillie of Aberdeen, and his wife Marjory Menzies, birth brief issued in 1648. [APB]

FORBES, or GAUGIN or FORBES, LOUISA, wife of Carl F. W. Koch a merchant in Stettin, heir to her mother Jane Allison who died on 20 May 1860, widow of John James Gaugin a merchant in Edinburgh, 13 August 1868. [NRS.S/H]

FORBES, MATTIAS, Governor of Osnabruck, 1635. [MGIF.Map 3]

FORBES, ROBERT, professed at the Monastery of St James, Wurzburg, by 1614, matriculated at Wurzburg on 12 March 1629, later Abbot from 1636 to 1637. [SF#272, 279]

FORBES, WALTER, son of James Forbes and his wife Margaret Black in Round Lichnet, Aberdeenshire, emigrated from Aberdeen to Danzig, in 1696, a merchant in Columne, Prussia, birth brief issued in 1705. [APB]

FORBES, Colonel WILLIAM, governor of Burg at Bremen-Verden, 1649 to 1657. [MGIF.61; map 3]

FORBES, ….., daughter of Major Forbes, was born in Wiesbaden on 19 April 1859. [S#1199]

FORDMAN, OTTO, valet de chamber to the Duke of Argyll, was admitted as a burgess of Glasgow on 6 January 1716. [GBR]

FORFAR, WILLIAM, eldest son of William Forfar in Gripsoball/Grapswall (Greifswald?) in Pomerland,(Pomerania), serviced as heir to his father's brother James Forfar in Scotstoun of Powburn, Kincardineshire, on 21 October 1656; also a sasine in Kincardineshire dated 31 May 1657. [NRS.RS6.52]

FORSYTH, ALEXANDER, at the Ratisbon Seminary in 1748.
[SIG#295][RSC#I.252]

FOSCHE, CLAUS, skipper of the King David of Hamburg, a
bond, 1683. [NRS.RD3.55.183]

FRAME, DAVID GEORGE, an accountant from Glasgow,
married Martha Renowitzey, eldest daughter of Wilhelm
Renowitzey, in Berlin on 21 October 1873. [GH#10552]

FRASER, ALEXANDER, was at the Ratisbon Seminary in 1800.
[SIG#295] [RSC#I.254]

FRASER, ANDREW, son of Alaster Fraser of Glenshee and his
wife Elspeth Spalding, a traveller in Lutzo, (Butzoe,
Mecklenburg?), Dundee birth brief dated 13 July 1616.
[Dundee Burgh Archives]

FRASER, CHARLES, was at Ratisbon Seminary in 1756.
[SIG#295][RSC#I.252]

FRASER, CHARLES H., in Hamburg, reports, 1796.
[NRS.NRAS#3955/60/2/165; 60/1/449]

FRASER, CHARLES, was at the Ratisbon Seminary in 1800, a
Catholic missionary in Aberdeen around 1830. [SIG#295]
[RSC#I.254]

FRASER, COLUMBANUS, from Buchan, professed at the
Monastery of St James in Wurzburg in 1667, possibly died
in 1677. [SF#280]

FRASER, HENRY, in Hamburg, letters, 1798.
[NRS.NRAS#3955/60/1/17, 44]

FRASER, JAMES, born 1831, youngest son of Hugh James
Fraser, a Lieutenant of the 2nd Dragoons (King of Bavaria's
Regiment), in Austrian service, died at Monasteryska,
Gallicia, on 26 March 1855. [W.XVI.1641]

FRASER, WILLIAM, of Phopachie, MD, physician to His Imperial Majesty, testament confirmed with the Commissariat of Edinburgh on 15 February 1752. [NRS]

FRAZER CHARLOTTE D., in Vienna, probate 15 January 1824, Prob.11/1688 PCC

FREER, ADAM, in Bremen, 1683. [NRS.RH15.106.494]

FULLARTON JOHN, of Dudwick, a soldier in France and Germany, a Lieutenant Colonel under Colonel Alexander Erskine brother to the Earl of Mar, a Colonel from 1640 to 1645. [NRS.NRAS.0107.8]

FYEN, GILBERT, son of Robert Fyen, a burgess of Aberdeen, and his wife Janet Lumsden, died in "Sanctanaberie", Saxony, in September 1599. [APB]

GADEBUACH, DORIS, born 1820 in Meikelburg, Germany, a servant in Edinburgh by 1851. [Census]

GALL, ALEXANDER, born in Aberdeen on 15 July 1836, was at the Ratisbon Seminary from 1852 to 1855, died in Aberdeen on 21 February 1872. [SIG#296][RSC#I.258]

GARDEN, ALEXANDER, a Major of the Swedish Army, 1635-1653, Governor of Brux and Dupau, 1646. [MGIF.Map 3]

GARDEN, JOHN, born 7 February 1825, was at the Ratisbon Seminary in 1838, returned to Scotland in 1840, died in Elgin, Morayshire, in 1863. [SIG#295][RSC#I.256]

GARDYNE, Captain GEORGE, in Germany, son of Alexander Gardyne of Banchory and his wife Janet Strachan, birth brief issued in 1639. [APB]

GARDYNE, JOHN, son of Andrew Gardyne and his wife Helen walker in Cambrokie, Tarves, Aberdeenshire, a traveller in Pomerania, 1593. [APB]

GARIOCH, ROBERT, educated at the Braunsberg Seminary around 1617.later in Rome. [SIG#299]

GARTERAR, JOHN, born 1817 in Neustadt, Baden, a watchmaker and artist in Edinburgh by 1851. [Census]

GATLINGER, S., born 1765 in Berlin, Prussia, arrived in Great Britain in 1783, a portrait painter in the Linenhall, Canongate, Edinburgh, by 1798. [ECA.SL115.2.1/53]

GAUDIE, ANDREW, of Craigmuie, Balmaclellan, Galloway, ambassador to Prince Ragozzi of Hungary in Hamburg after 1641, later by 1660 a Major General in the service of the Elector of Brandenburg, died as Andreas von Gaudy in 1665. [SGen.LIII.2/51][SIG#288]

GEDDES, ANDREW, from Cairnfield, a monk at the Scots Monastery at Wurzburg, 1785. [SIG#304]

GEDDES, PLACIDUS, from Edinburgh, a monk at the Scots Monastery at Wurzburg, 1785; former Prior of the Scottish Monastery at Wurzburg, 1832. [SiG#304][NRS.NRAS.3250/32]

GERARD, JOHN, youngest son of the late Lieutenant Colonel Gerard of Rochsoles, Lanarkshire, died in Graz on 31 December 1858. [W.XX.2051]

GIBSON, ALEXANDER CAMPBELL, a merchant in Hamburg, inventory, 21 May 1847, with the Commissariat of Edinburgh. [NRS]

GIBSON, DAVID, member of the Scottish Brotherhood at Greifswald, around 1600. [SIG#315]

GIBSON, JAMES, son of Sir Alexander Gibson of Pentland and his wife Helen Fleming, settled in Austria during 1716, Lieutenant Colonel of Horse who served in the Hungarian wars. [NNQ.IV.81]

GIBSON, WILLIAM, a merchant in Hamburg, inventory, 12 December 1864, with the Commissariat of Edinburgh. [NRS]

GILBERT, JOHN, a merchant in Hamburg, 1652. [NRS.GD57.336.10]

GILES, JAMES, and his wife in Dresden, 1871. [NRS.RD5.1397.497]

GILLESPIE, WILLIAM, from the Diocese of Aberdeen, matriculated at the University of Koln in 1443. [SNQ.X.3/44]

GLOYSTEIN, BARENT, in Bremen, despatched the St Francis of Bremen to Edinburgh in 1699. [NRS.RH15.14.74]

GOGEL, JOHN, from Frankfurt am Main, was admitted as a burgess and guildsbrother of Edinburgh on 21 October 1744. [EBR]

GOGEL, PETER, from Frankfurt am Main, was admitted as a burgess and guildsbrother of Edinburgh on 8 April 1752. [EBR]

GORDON, ADAM, born 1611, as Captain of Colonel Munro's regiment, sailed from Cromarty to Hamburg in 1631, died at the Battle of Nordlingen on 27 August 1634. [HG#1637]

GORDON, ADAM, son of the late Sir Adam Gordon of Parke, a Captain of Colonel Leslie's regiment in Swedish service in Germany, 1638. [NRS.RH15.16.27a][SIG#283]

GORDON, ALEXANDER, was educated at the Scots College in Rome from 1657 to 1658, then a Benedictine in Germany. [SF#275]

GORDON, ALEXANDER, at the Ratisbon Seminary in 1718. [SIG#294][RSC#I.250]

GORDON, ALEXANDER, from Dorleathers, at the Ratisbon Seminary in 1719. [SIG#294][RSC#I.251]

GORDON, ALEXANDER, of Licheston, at the Ratisbon Seminary in 1739. [SIG#294][RSC#I.252]

GORDON, ALEXANDER, brother of George Gordon in Fochabers, Morayshire, a captain in Prussian Service, 1744. [HG#1664]

GORDON, ALEXANDER, born in Upper Clachan of Enzie on 20 June 1829, was at the Ratisbon Seminary from 1841 to 1843. [SIG#295][RSC#I.256]

GORDON, ANDREW, was admitted to the Monastery of Ratisbon on 24 February 1732. [SIG#294]

GORDON, ANDREW, 3rd Count of Gordon, Adjutant General in Bohemia before 1754. [HG#1674]

GORDON, ANS., son of Alexander Gordon in Kinquidy, Diocese of Aberdeen, was admitted to the Monastery of Ratisbon on 25 March 1682, died 1702. [SIG#293]

GORDON, ANSELM, born 1672, professed in the Monastery of Wurzburg in 1689, died 1730. [SF#281]

GORDON, ARTHUR, born 1731, son of Lord Baldony, at the Ratisbon Seminary in 1739. [SIG#294][RSC#I.252]

GORDON, AUGUSTINE, matriculated at Wurzburg in September 1686, studied theology and canon law. [SF#272]

GORDON, CHARLES, of Baldorny, born 5 March 1737, matriculated at the Ratisbon Seminary in 1748. [SIG#295][RSC#I.252]

GORDON, CHARLES, a Lieutenant Colonel in Prussian Service, 1790. [NRS.GD38.2.30]

GORDON, EDWARD STRATHNAIRN, infant son of F.J. and E.A.Gordon, died in Axenfels, Switzerland, on 2 August 1884. [EC#31167]

GORDON, FRANCIS, a student at the University of Rostock in 1615. [SIG#313]

GORDON, GEORGE, in Stuttgart, 1833. [NRS.GD66.2.12]

GORDON, GILBERT, a student at the Scots College in Douai around 1626-1634, a Benedictine in Germany between 1636 and 1640. [SF#274]

GORDON, H, from the Diocese of Aberdeen, was admitted to the Monastery of Ratisbon on 2 February 1667, died 1674. [SIG#293]

GORDON, J., (1627-1657), a soldier in the service of the Grand Duke of Hesse. [HG#1750]

GORDON, JANE CHARLOTTE, of Lesmore, Convent of St Anne in Munich, 1842. [NRS.NRAS.3250/22]

GORDON, Reverend JOHAN PHILIP, clerk of Bissendorf, probate 20 March 1844. [NA.Prob.11/1995]

GORDON, JOHN, of Craichlaw, soldier in Germany under Lord Spynie, 1631. [RPCS.IV.371]

GORDON, JOHN, son of John Gordon, an officer of the army of the Emperor of Austria, captured by the Swedes at Nuremberg in November 1631, died in Danzig during December 1648. [HG#1753]

GORDON, JOHN, Governor of Eger, 1632. [MGIF.Map 3]

GORDON, JOHN HENRY, born 1815, son of Edward Gordon of Lesmoir, in Austrian service. [HG#1775]

GORDON, MARJORY, daughter of Patrick Gordon the younger

of Kincraigie, Aberdeenshire, and his wife Elizabeth Gordon, emigrated to Germany with a birth brief during 1637. [APB]

GORDON, PATRICK, a student at the University of Rostock in 1589. [SIG#313]

GORDON, PATRICK, of Letterfury, at the Ratisbon Seminary, 1718. [RSC#I.250]

GORDON, ROBERT, at the Ratisbon Seminary in 1719. [SIG#294][RSC#I.250]

GORDON, WILLIAM, born after 1560, son of the 5th Earl of Huntly, student at the Scots College in Douai around 1594, and was a monk at Wurzburg, died in Paris on 14 September 1638. [SF#274, 279]

GORDON, WILLIAM, at the Ratisbon Seminary in 1713. [SIG#294][RSC#I.250]

GORDON, ..., Colonel, at Lubeck, 1648. [Testament in NRS.Misc. Executry pp]

GORDON, ..., of Mackay's Regiment, was killed at Stalsund, Prussia, in June 1628. [HG#1622]

GOTTLIEFF-BILDZINDS, JOHAN, a goldsmith, was admitted as a burgess and guilds-brother of Glasgow on 18 June 1716. [GBR]

GOUT, OTTO, a merchant in Hamburg, 1692. [NRS.AC7.9]

GRAEME, or GIERSBURG, Mrs AMELIA ANN MARGARET, daughter of the deceased Major George Drummond Graeme of Inchbrakie, and wife of Lieutenant Arived Giersburg of the Prussian Service, a certificate, 10 March 1876. [NRS.Lyon Office, GIII.29]

GRAHAM, CHARLES, was at Ratisbon Seminary in 1779, was

living in London by 1844. [SIG#295][RSC#I.253]

GRAHAM, JOHN, a merchant burgess in 'Rostinebrege' in the Duchy of Spruce, (Prussia), testament confirmed with the Commissariat of Edinburgh on 8 February 1622. [NRS]

GRAHAM, NINIAN, born 1639, professed at the Monastery of St James, Wurzburg, in 1665, died in Scotland before April 1680. [SF#280]

GRAHAM, THOMAS, born on 11 August 1766, was at Ratisbon Seminary in 1775. [SIG#295][RSC#I.253]

GRANT, ALEXANDER, at the Ratisbon Seminary in 1718. [SIG#294][RSC#I.250]

GRANT, ALEXANDER, at the Ratisbon Seminary in 1739. [SIG#294][RSC#I.252]

GRANT, CALUM, from Strathdon, son of the Laird of Ruthven, was admitted to the Monastery of Ratisbon on 1 November 1721. [SIG#293]

GRANT, CATHERINE, wife of Reverend David Edward the Free Church missionary to the Jews, died in Breslau, Prussia, on 21 January 1861. [W.XXII.2279]

GRANT, E., from Strathdon, was admitted to the Monastery of Ratisbon on 1 November 1720. [SIG#293]

GRANT, JOHN, of Blairfindy, matriculated at the Ratisbon Seminary in 1748. [SIG#295][RSC#I.252]

GRANT, JOHN, was at Ratisbon Seminary in 1764. [SIG#295][RSC#I.253]

GRANT, JOHN, second son of Duncan Grant, Newhall House, Lanarkshire, married Olga Matilda Alexandrina, baroness Wegner, in Weimar on 23 November 1848. [EEC#21744]

GRANT, KIL., from Strathspey, was admitted to the Monastery of Ratisbon on 30 November 1709. [SIG#293]

GRANT, LUDOVICK, at the Ratisbon Seminary 1718. [SIG#294][RSC#I.250]

GRANT, MAURICE, from Strathdon, son of the laird of Auchlichny, was admitted to the Monastery of Ratisbon on 5 October 1724. [SIG#293]

GRANT, ROBERT, at the Ratisbon Seminary in 1713. [SIG#294]

GRANT, ROBERT, the younger, at the Ratisbon Seminary in 1713. [SIG#294][RSC#I.250]

GRANT, ROBERT, at the Ratisbon Seminary in 1719. [SIG#294][RSC#I.250]

GRANT, ROBERT, matriculated at the Ratisbon Seminary in 1735. [RSC#I/251]

GRANT, WILLIAM, at the Ratisbon Seminary in 1713. [SIG#294][RSC#I.250]

GRANT, Professor WILLIAM, at the Ratisbon Seminary in 1713. [SIG#294][RSC#I.249]

GRANT, ..., of Dunlugas, Banffshire, an officer in the army of Elizabeth, Empress of Russia, later a Major General in the service of Frederick the Great of Prussia, Governor of Neisse, Silesia, in 1763, died there in 1764. [SIG#288]

GRAY, Colonel Sir ANDREW, sailed from Leith bound for Hamburg with 1500 recruits for service under the King of Bohemia in 1620. [RPCS.XII.lxxviii][STW#111]

GRAY, ANDREW, from Dundee, admitted to the Monastery of Ratisbon on 21 March 1641, died in Poland during 1695. [SIG#292]

GRAY, D., in Hamburg, 1796. [NRS.NRAS#3955/60/1/452]

GRAY, GILBERT, a student at the University of Helmstadt in 1593. [SIG#313]

GRAY, JOACHIM, born 1715 in Fochabers, Morayshire, was admitted to the Monastery of Ratisbon on 4 October 1739. [SIG#294]

GRAY, WILLIAM, was educated at the Scots College in Rome from 1653 to 1656, then a monk in Germany. [SF#275]

GREEN, PETER, educated at the Braunsberg Seminary around 1586, became a Jesuit and taught philosophy at Graz. [SIG#299]

GREENLEES, [Grinlis], JOHN, a shopkeeper in Strasburg, Western Prussia, 1573. [SIG#51]

GREGG, JOHN, [Hans Grigge], in Anklam, near Greifswald, 1623. [Anklam Baptismal Register]

GRISON, WILLIAM, a merchant in Hamburg from 1640s. [StH. Genealogische Sammlungen, 741-2, Die Fremden in den Rechnungsbuchern de Wedde und Kammerei]

GRUNING, HERMAN, in Bremen, 1601. [SD.2.327]

GUNN, JOHN, born in October 1608, a member of the family of Gunn of Golspie, a Colonel in Swedish service, fought in Germany, Governor of Ohlau in Silesia in 1638, married a Miss von Arnim, died on 9 April 1649 and buried in Ohlau, Silesia. [SIG#283/316]

GUNN, W., a Captain of the Swedish Army in Germany during the 1630s, afterwards a Colonel and General in Imperial Service. [SIG#283]

GUENTHER, or ZAHN, ELEANORA, in Stainshanan, Bohemia, heir to her granduncle Henry Strobach a glasscutter in Leith, 3 April 1828. [NRS.S/H]

GUENTHER, or ZAHN, JANE, in Stainshanan, Bohemia, heir to her granduncle Henry Strobach a glasscutter in Leith, 3 April 1828. [NRS.S/H]

GUENTHER, or ZAHN, JOSEPHA, in Stainshanan, Bohemia, heir to her granduncle Henry Strobach a glasscutter in Leith, 3 April 1828. [NRS.S/H]

GUENTHER, or STELZIG, TERESA, in Stainshanan, Bohemia, heir to her granduncle Henry Strobach a glasscutter in Leith, also to his widow Charlotte Hector in Leith, 3 April 1828. [NRS.S/H]

GUENTHER, or GROSSMAN, TERESA, in Stainshanan, Bohemia, heir to her guncle Henry Strobach a glasscutter in Leith, also to Charlotte Hector, his widow in Leith, 3 April 1828. [NRS.S/H]

GUNTHER, ALBERT, born 1832 in Saxony, a painter journeyman in Edinburgh by 1851. [Census]

GUNTHER, JULIUS, born 1824 in Saxony, a painter journeyman in Edinburgh by 1851. [Census]

'GUTTERN, ANDREAS', in Anklam, near Greifswald, 1608-1623. [HKA]

HAGART, SUSAN, born 1827, youngest daughter of Thomas C. Hagart of Bantaskine, died in Augsburg, Bavaria, on 4 July 1841. [W.II.158]

HAIG, MARGARET, second daughter of William Haig, and grand-daughter of Robert Haig of Seggie, died in Arosa, Switzerland, on 16 January 1898. [S#17021]

HALDANE, GEORGE, in Cassell, 1717. [NRS.GD24/2/5/195]

HALIBURTON, Major THOMAS, Governor of Steinburg,

1658; commander of Steinburg, north of Hamburg, 1660. [MGIF.22; Map 3]

HALIDAY, THOMAS, a brasier, was sent to Hamburg by Edinburgh Town Council in 1649. [EBR: 28 March 1649]

HALLIWELL, JOHN, a trainer in Voslaw, Austria, an inventory, 1874. [NRS.SC70.166/699]

HAMILTON, Sir ALEXANDER, of Innerwick, Captain of Nithsdale's regiment, raised a company of men in Ireland which he shipped from Scotland to Germany in 1628. [RPCS.II.241]

HAMILTON, ALEXANDER, Governor of Hanau, 1631-1634. [MGIF.Map 3]

HAMILTON, ALEXANDER, was at Ratisbon Seminary in 1764. [SIG#295][RSC#I.253]

HAMILTON, ANDREW, a merchant in Prussia, dead by 1655, brother of Archibald Hamilton a merchant burgess of Edinburgh, [RGS.X.374]; a merchant in 'Spruce and Poll' (Prussia and Poland) in 1664. [NRS.RD2.11.538]

HAMILTON, Dr ANDREW, of Geneva, was admitted as a burgess and guildsbrother of Ayr on 12 October 1695. [ABR]

HAMILTON, ARCHIBALD, from Edinburgh, a merchant in Prussia around 1655. [RGS.X.374]

HAMILTON, FRANCIS, from Edinburgh, a student at the Scots College in Douai in 1587, matriculated at Wurzburg 13 August 1596, and by 1598 was a monk at Ratisbon, Abbot of Wurzburg 1602-1605, died after 1617 possibly at Kirchworbis. [SF#272-274-279]

HAMILTON, FREDERICK, Standard bearer to Augustus of Norway, Duke of Slesvig-Holstein, Vice General of the

Elector of Brandenburg, 1665. [EUL: Laing.ms#2589]

HAMILTON, HUGH, Governor of Greifswald, 1646.
[MGIF.Map 3]

HAMILTON, JAMES, Marquis of Hamilton, General of the
Swedish Army in Germany, 1630s, at the Siege of
Magdeburg in 1632. [SIG#282][NRS.GD406.1.9368]

HAMILTON, Sir J.,a Colonel of the Swedish Army in Germany
during the 1630s. [SIG#283]

HAMILTON, JAMES, at the Ratisbon Seminary in 1713.
[SIG#294][RSC#I.250]

HAMILTON, JAMES, born 18 October 1752, was at Ratisbon
Seminary in 1764. [SIG#295][RSC#I.253]

HAMILTON, JOHN, in Hanover, 1723. [NRS.GD158.1299]

HAMILTON, PLACIDUS, was admitted to the Monastery of
Ratisbon on 30 November 1709. [SIG#293]

HAMILTON, ..., a Colonel of the Swedish Army in Germany
during the 1630s. [SIG#283]

HAMILTON, Lieutenant Colonel, Deputy Governor of
Heligoland, 1811. [NRS.GD51.6.1787]

HAMPTON, ROBERT, son of ..... Hampton in Balhagartie, was
recruited by David Ramsay, servant of Sir Alexander
Strachan of Thornton, to serve as a soldier in Germany, in
1626, died at Gluckstadt in 1627. [RPCS.II.80, 343]

HARDY, JOHN, born in Glasgow on 9 June 1840, was at the
Ratisbon Seminary in 1852. [SIG#296] [RSC#I.258]

HARRINGTON, JAMES, a merchant in Hamburg, 1652.
[NRS.GD57.336.10]

HARVEY, [Herve], ANDREW, settled in Mewe, Western Prussia, in 1578. [SIG#51]

HAUNSHEILL, HENRY, master of the <u>City of Hamburg</u>, 1674. [NRS.AC7.4]

HAUPTMAN, ..., daughter of Franz Hauptman, was born at Greenside Cottage, Edinburgh, on 8 February 1856. [W.XVII.1735]

HAY, ALEXANDER, educated at the Braunsberg Seminary around 1642, returned to Scotland. [SIG#299]

HAY, ALEXANDER, in Hamburg pre 1644, brother of James and Patrick. [NRS.RH9.5.22]

HAY, Mrs ANN, in Germany, 1847. [NRS.RD5.790.305]

HAY, BENEDICT, of Dalgetty, from Wurzburg to Ratisbon in 1673. [SF#280]

HAY, JOHN, educated at the Braunsberg Seminary around 1642. [SIG#299]

HAY, JOHN, died in Baden-Baden on 17 November 1845. [NRS.S/H]

HEATLEY, G., a Captain of the Swedish Army in Germany during the 1630s. [SIG#283]

HECTOR, JOHN, a fishcurer from Wick, in Hamburg, 1821. [NRS.CS17.40.646]

HEDDLE, EMILY, possibly from Orkney, in Wildbad, Wurtemburg, 1845. [NRS.GD263/97]

HEGATE, JAMES, born around 1601 in Glasgow, a student at the Scots College in Douai, who went to Wurzburg in 1623, possibly died in May 1631. [SF#274, 279]

HEGGIE, (?), {"HEGECK"}, **ARCHIBALD,** educated at the Braunsberg Seminary around 1613. [SIG#299]

HEIDENSOHN, CHRISTIAN CARL FRIEDRICH, Wilsmarck, Prussia, inventory, 8 December 1864, with the Commissariat of Edinburgh. [NRS]

HEINRIKSON, HANS, a merchant in Hamburg, 1674. [NRS.AC7.5]

HEMELINGK, GERDT, a citizen of Bremen, and a merchant at Drosteness, Shetland Islands, 1567. [SD.1.166]

HEMLIN, GERARD, a shipmaster from Bremen, in Shetland, 1567. [SD.1.171]

HENDERSON, JOHN, in Hamburg, 1638. [NRS.GD406.1.10805]

HENDERSON, JOHN, at the Ratisbon Seminary in 1719. [SIG#294][RSC#I.251]

HENDERSON, OLYMPIA, in Campagne, Lausanne, probate 9 May 1843, Prob.11/1979 PCC

HENNIKER, WILLIAM, born 1748 in Hanover, a stay and habit-maker, emigrated to London in 1769, resident of 5 George Street, Edinburgh, by 1798. [SCA.SL115.2.1/39]

HENRYSON, ROBERT, a student at the University of Greifswald in 1596, later at Frankfurt-on-the Oder in 1598. [SIG#313/314]

HEPBURN, JAMES, a student at Frankfurt-on-the Oder in 1587. [SIG#313]

HEPBURN Sir JOHN, born 1598, second son of George Hepburn of Athelstaneford in East Lothian, educated at Marischal College, Aberdeen, in the service of Frederick of Bohemia from 1620-1623, a Swedish Army Colonel from

1625-1632, entered the service of Bernard of Weimar during 1635, died at the Siege of Saverne on 8 July 1636, testament confirmed with the Commissariat of Edinburgh on 1 June 1638. [SHR.IX.49]; Governor of Landshut, 1631-1632. [MGIF.Map 3][SIG#283]

HEPBURN, WILLIAM, born 17 December 1826, was at the Ratisbon Seminary in 1838, returned to Scotland in 1848. [SIG#295][RSC#I.256]

HEROCH, MOSES, born during 1781 in Scholarke, Prussia, later in Hamburg, a merchant, residing at 6 Register Street, Edinburgh, by April 1817. [ECA.SL115.2.2/78]

HERRIES, KILIAN, born 1663, professed at the Monastery of Wurzburg in 1679, died 30 March 1683. [SF#280]

HERZFELDER, GOTTLIEB AMADEUS, from Pesth, died at sea, inventory, 26 August 1848, with the Commissariat of Edinburgh. [NRS]

HERTZOG, HERMAN, master of the Goldstern of Bremen, at Aberdeen on 25 August 1665. [ACA.ASW.530]

HESSE, CHARLES, born 1786 in Berlin, a student, arrived in Leith on 16 August 1801, residing in Thomson's Lodgings, St Andrew Street, Edinburgh, in 1803. [ECA.SL115.2.1/146]

HILL, ROBERT, a student at the Scots College in Douai around 1593, and by 1598 was a monk at Ratisbon. [SF#274]

HINSH, JOACHIM, a merchant in Hamburg, a bond, 1680. [NRS.RD4.47.841]

HINSMAN, JOACHIM, a merchant in Hamburg, a bond, 1670. [NRS.RD3.25.106]

HIRSCHEL, Sir WILLIAM, born in Hanover on 15 November 1738, an astronomer, graduated LL.D. from the University of Glasgow in 1792, died in Slough, Windsor, England, in 1822. [RGG]

HODGKIN, Mrs ELIZA, born in Linden, Hanover, in 1796, wife of M. Hodgkin, Royal Navy, residing at 5 Buccleugh Street, Edinburgh, by 4 August 1819. [ECA.SL115.2.2/89]

HOFFMAN, AUGUSTINE, a German soldier-of-fortune who served as the quartermaster of Leslie's Horse in the Army of the Solemn League and Covenant around 1644-1647, Captain of Hoffman's Horse 1650-1651, fled to Norway in January 1652. [RHCA#376]

HOG, JOHN, a student at the University of Heidelberg, matriculated on 8 October 1611. [SIG#314][SHR.V.67][RCPE]

HOG, ROBERT, son of John Hog a minister in Rotterdam 1660s, settled in Luneburg in 1684. [NRS.GD26.13.492]

HOME, DAVID, of Caldra, a soldier in Germany around 1758. [NRS.GD267.1.4]

HOMEYER, ..., son of Frederick Homeyer, was born in Ranzin, Pomerania, on 6 February 1859. [S#1139]

HOPTING, ANTON, born 1768 in the Schwartzwald, a wooden clockmaker, emigrated from Hamburg to Leith, settled in the Lawnmarket, Edinburgh, around 1790. [ECA.SL115.2.1/40]

HORN, ALEXANDER, born 28 June 1762, was at Ratisbon Seminary in 1772. [SIG#295][RSC#I.253]

HORN, JAMES, born in Montrose, Angus, on 25 July 1765, was at Ratisbon Seminary in 1779, died in Germany on 2 April 1833. [SIG#295][RSC#I.254]

HORNE, GEORGE, son of Alexander Horne and his wife Margaret Innes in Boyne, Ferdraught, a resident of Bublitz,

Pomerania, 1594. [APB]

HORROREN, JOHN, a merchant in the Dukedom of Spruce, 1664. [NRS.RD2.10.914]

HORSANET, HANS, was admitted as a burgess of the Canongate on 16 July 1663. [CBR]

HOUGH, GEORGE, married Marie Young in the English Church of Hamburg on 21 February 1656. [TKH]

HOWIE, ROBERT, a student at the University of Rostock in 1584. [SIG#313]

HOWIE, WILLIAM, a priest from the Diocese of Aberdeen, matriculated at the University of Koln in 1469. [SNQ.X.3/78]

HUCHEON, ARTHUR, son of William Hucheon and his wife Helen Philip in Leither, Turriff, Aberdeenshire, a traveller in Prussia, 1599. [APB]

HUDTWALCKER, AUGUSTE CAROLINE, third daughter of Senator Hudtwalcker of Hamburg, married George C. Bruce, in Hamburg on 20 May 1857. [W.XVIII.1874]
HUGHAN, THOMAS, of Airds, married Lady Louisa Georgina Beauclerk, sister of the Duke of St Albans, in Munich, 1836. [DPCA#1747]

HUICK, HENRY, master of the Sea Ryder of Bremen, a charter party re a voyage from Scotland to France in 1657. [NRS.GD150.2535.1]

HUISHE, JOIHIM, a merchant in Hamburg, a bond, 1675. [NRS.RD3.40.34]

HUME, or **WEMYSS, ROBERT,** matriculated at the University of Heidelberg on 22 February 1593. [SHR.V.67]

HUME, ROBERT, a Captain of the Swedish Army in Germany

during the 1630s. [SIG#283]

HUNTER, ANDREW, [Andreas Hunter], in Anklam, near Greifswald, 1687-1700. [HKA]

HUNTER, ARCHIBALD, a student at the University of Rostock in 1588. [SIG#313]

HUNTER, WILLIAM, many years at the flax department of Grandholm Mills, late an employee of Richards and Company at the Broadford Works, Aberdeen, died in Memel, Prussia, on 14 January 1850. [AJ#5325]

INDEMMS, FERDINAND, born 1791 in Gratz, a gentleman, landed at Harwich on 20 December 1816, residing at 37 North Frederick Street, Edinburgh, by November 1817. [ECA.SL115.2.2/81]

INGLIS, MUNGO, in Heidelberg, also in Hamburg, 1689. [NRS.RH15.109.689] {Possibly Mungo Inglis, born 1657, educated at Edinburgh University, a tutor at the College of William and Mary, Virginia, from 1694 to 1705, died 1719 (WMQ#6/87)}

INGLIS, S. B., of the German Legion, 1812. [NRS.RD5.361.656]

INGRAM, ALEXANDER, educated at the Braunsberg Seminary around 1613. [SIG#299]

INGRAM, BEN., from Rothes, a monk at the Scots Monastery at Wurzburg in 1791. [SIG#304]

INNES, Sir J., a Colonel of the Swedish Army in Germany during the 1630s. [SIG#283]

INNES, JOHN, a Captain of the Swedish Army in Germany during the 1630s, died at Stralsund. [SIG#283]

INNES, JOHN, a merchant in Hamburg, was admitted as a burgess of Montrose in 1730. [MBR]

INNES, P., a Captain of the Swedish Army in Germany during the 1630s, died at Nurnberg. [SIG#283]

IRVINE, JAMES MARIANUS, possibly of Belty, at Wurzburg on 28 July 1685, abbot from 1685 to 1688, died 22 November 1688. [SF#280]

IRVINE, RICHARD, born in Stackheugh, Dumfries-shire, professed at Ratisbon after 1580, Abbot of Erfurt 1585-1595, Abbot of Wurzburg 1595-1598, died after 30 December 1626 either in Ratisbon or Kelheim. [SF#279]

IRVINE, ROBERT FRANCIS, was educated at the Scots College at Douai in 1633, then a monk in Germany, returned to Douai in 1639, a monk in Wurzburg after May 1643, then became a Capuchin. [SF#274]

IRVING, ALEXANDER, Governor of Regensburg, 1633. [MGIF.Map 3]

IRVING, Colonel ALEXANDER, Governor of Stade ca.1655. [MGIF.70; map 3]

IRVING, EDWARD, son of John Irving in Borwick, Orkney, settled in Lubeck, Germany, by 1636. [NRS.RS43.5.230]

ISLES, ANDREW BURTON, elder son of Andrew Isles a merchant in Edinburgh, died in Eisenach, Saxe-Weimar, on 3 March 1879. [S#11,118]

IDLEWIND, JANE WANNAN, 4th daughter of John Idlewind sugar baker, born in Reghan, Germany, and his wife Jane, daughter of Henry Shanks invalid in Dundee, born 25 May, baptised 30 May 1813 in Dundee. [St Paul's Episcopal Cathedral Baptismal Register]

JACK, ANDREW, educated at the Braunsberg Seminary around 1582, later in Vienna. [SIG#298]

JACK, ANDREW, a small trader in Wismar about 1600.

[SIG#51]

JACK, ANDREW, a student at the University of Rostock in
1609. [SIG#313]

JACKSON, Sir KEITH ALEXANDER, late Captain of the 4th
Light Dragoons, died in Schlierbach, Heidelberg, on 21 July
1843. [GA#5933]

JAMIESON, JOHN, a suspected priest who had returned to
Scotland from Ratisbon or Windsburg, was imprisoned in
Aberdeen Tolbooth in 1690. [RPCS.XVI.469]

JANSEN, HEINRICH, master of St John the Baptist of
Hamburg, 1627. [NRS.AC1.60, 92]

JANSEN, JAN, bosun of the Nightingale of Hamburg, 1627.
[NRS.AC7.1.2]

JOCKEL, CATHERINE, born 1821 in Bavaria, settled in
Edinburgh by 1851. [Census]

JOCKEL, CHRISTIAN, born 1811 in Germany, a
warehouseman in Edinburgh by 1851, and his wife
Catherine, born 1817 in Germany. [Census]

JOHNSON, ["IANSEN"], DAVID, married Anna Dirx, a widow,
in Hamburg in 1609. [TKH]

JOHNSTON, ARTHUR, from Aberdeen, a student at the
University of Heidelberg, matriculated on 11 September
1599. [SIG#314][SHR.V.67][RCPE]

JOHNSTON, JOHN, born 1570, educated at King's College,
Aberdeen, a student at the University of Rostock in 1584,
and at the University of Heidelberg in 1587, by 1593 he was
Professor of Divinity at St Andrews University, died in
1611. [SIG#313/314][SHR.V.67][RCPE]

JOHNSTON, JOHN, son of Andrew Johnston and his wife

Margaret Stern in Carnfochie, Tarves, Aberdeenshire, died in Stralsund before 1592. [APB]

JOHNSTON, JOHN, in Berlin, 1710, bound for Russia. [NRS.GD27.3.2]

JOHNSTON, THOMAS, was educated at the Scots College in Madrid in 1647, a monk in Ratisbon from 1655. [SF#275]

JOHNSTON, WILLIAM, a student at the University of Heidelberg, matriculated on 26 February 1603. [SIG#314][SHR.V.67]

JOHNSTONE, ARTHUR, from Aberdeen, a student at the University of Helmstadt in 1599, then an academic in Heidelburg, 1599-1601. [SIG#311/313]

JOHNSTONE, ELIZA HOPE, in Zofingen, Switzerland, inventory, 11 November 1864, with the Commissariat of Edinburgh. [NRS]

JOHNSTONE, JAMES, a student at the University of Helmstadt in 1585. [SIG#313]

JOHNSTONE, Sir JAMES, of Elphinstone, a captain of the Duke of Lunenburg's army, 1677. [NRS.GD190.3.195]

JOHNSTON, MARY JOSEPHA, from Perth, with her children, in Bavaria, 1857. [NRS.NRAS.3250/50]

JOHNSTONE, NINIAN, from the Diocese of Aberdeen, was admitted to the Monastery of Ratisbon on 6 May 1655. [SIG#292]

JOLLY, ROBERT, a merchant in Hamburg, deeds, letters, 1683, 1697,1698. [NRS.RD2.62.369; RD4.80.61; RD2.81/1.447, 741; RD2.81/2.434; RH15.106.689.17; RH15/140]; testament confirmed on 1 July 1714 with the Commissariat of Edinburgh. [NRS]

JOXHEIM, JOBST WILLIAM, possibly from Hamburg, was admitted as a burgess of Glasgow on 3 June 1735. [GBR]

KAY, THOMAS, son of John Kay and his wife Katherine Selby in Gardyne, Aberdeenshire, died in Melvin, Prussia, in 1587. [APB]

KEITH, DAVID PLACID, matriculated at Wurzburg on 18 November 1654, studied logic, possibly in Poland by 1662. [SF#272-279]

KEITH Field Marshal JAMES, born 1696 in Peterhead, Aberdeenshire, brother of the Earl Marischal, served as a soldier in Spain and Russia before becoming a Field Marshal under Frederick the Great of Prussia, died in 1758.

KEITH, Lady JANE, a widow in Berne, probate 7 April 1798, Prob.11/1305 PCC

KEITH, ROBERT, Lieutenant of the Kaporski Regiment, at Neyhausen, Bohemia, 1736. [NRS.NRAS#61, box 2, bundle 15]

KEITH, Sir R. MURRAY, in Vienna, 1787. [NRS.NRAS#1054, bundle 130]

KELLINGHUYSEN, GEORGE, partner of the <u>Nightingale of Bremen</u>, deeds, 1673. [NRS.RD3.33.721/724]

KELMAN, JAMES, born in Portsoy, Banffshire, on 3 April 1835, was at the Ratisbon Seminary in 1845-1848. [SIG#296] [RSC#I.257]

KENNEDY, LACHLAN, in Dusseldorf, a deed, 1859. [NRS.RD1081.350]

KENNEDY, PATRICK GEORGE, MD, Albany Street, Edinburgh, died in Hietzing, Vienna, inventory, 15 January 1838, with the Commissariat of Edinburgh. [NRS]

KENNEDY, ROBERT, Karlsruhe, probate 17 February 1844. [NA.Prob.11/1993]

KENNEDY, THOMAS, at the Ratisbon Seminary in 1719. [SIG#294]

KENNEDY, ILDEPHONSUS, was admitted to the Monastery of Ratisbon on 24 September 1742. [SIG#294]

KENNEDY, THOMAS, matriculated at the Ratisbon Seminary in 1735. [RSC#I.251]

KEPLE, Baron JOHN RABO, General of the Swiss, was admitted as a burgess and guildsbrother of Glasgow on 29 July 1719. [GBR]

KER, Miss MARY ANNE, daughter of William H. Ker of Kinninmont, died in Switzerland on 15 September 1851, inventory, 1854, Comm. Edinburgh. [NRS]

KEYSAR, MICHAEL, a paper maker at Dalry, 1595. [NRS.RD1.50.342]

KING, CHARLES, born 1762 in Hanover, a German teacher in Edinburgh by 1798. [ECA.SL115.2.1/54]

KING, Sir JAMES, a Major General of the Swedish Army in Germany, 1630s; Governor of Vlotho, 1637; a diplomat in Hamburg, 1639-1641. [MGIF.Map 3] [SSNE#2814][SIG#282]

KING, JAMES, the younger, a soldier in Hamburg, 1639. [SSNE#2815]

KINKELL, DIRECT, merchant of the Nightingale of Bremen, deeds, 1673. [NRS.RD3.33.726/727]

KINKLON, DIDERICK, a partner of the Nightingale of Bremen, deeds, 1673. [NRS.RD3.33.721/724]

KINLOCH, JOHN, servant of Walter Erskine in Grippiswald, 1614. [DSL]

KINNARD, DAVID, educated at the Braunsberg Seminary around 1599, became a Jesuit. [SIG#299]

KINNARD, PATRICK, educated at the Braunsberg Seminary around 1633. [SIG#299]

KINNEARD, JAMES, a student at the Scots College in Douai around 1620, later possibly a Benedictine in Germany. [SF#274]

KINNEIR, JOHN, born 1778 (?) in Neustadt, Black Forest, a wooden clockmaker who arrived in Leith and settled at West Bow, Edinburgh, by 1803. [ECA.SL115.2.2/15]

KINNEMOND, PATRICK, Governor of Anklam, 1638. [MGIF.Map 3]

KINNEMOND, THOMAS, Governor of Augsburg, 1632. [MGIF.Map 3]

KIRKALULEA, MARIE, born 1821 in Germany, a governess in Edinburgh by 1851. [Census]

KIRKCALDIE, GEORGE, born in Dunfermline in 1793, son of Thomas Kirkcaldie and his wife Mary Thomson, married in Bremen on 10 May 1815 to Hermanna Catherina Bredenkamp, born there on 20 May 1789.

KIRKHOFF, CHRISTIAN WILHELM, a merchant in Hamburg around 1730. [NRS.AC8/454]

KLOCHENHAUER, AUGUSTUS, in Edinburgh, 1871. [NRS.AD14.71.270]

KNAP, NICLAS, born in Hanover, a shipmaster in Dundee, husband of Janet Anderson born 1793, died 1811. [Howff gravestone, Dundee]

KNAPE, JOHN, a skipper trading between Wismar, Mecklenburg, and Scotland, 1563. [SIG#21]

KNIE, BALTHASER, born 1738 in Bohaven,(?), Germany, a weatherglass maker, settled in Cork, Ireland, then moved via Irvine to Edinburgh, in Lawnmarket, Edinburgh, around 1793. [ECA.SL115.2.1/30]

KNIGHT, JOHN KEPPEL, sometime of Jordanston in Perthshire, a Colonel in the Imperial Austrian Army, a genealogy, 29 May 1901. [NRS. Lyon Office]

KNOBLAUCH, CHRISTOPHER, a merchant in Prussia, was admitted as a guild burgess of Aberdeen on 22 August 1660. [Aberdeen Burgess Roll]

KNOPP, JANET JANE, first daughter of Nicholas Knopp, mariner aboard the <u>Good Trow of Liverpool,</u> a native of Bremen, Germany, and his wife Janet, daughter of John Anderson a farmer in Upper Claughan, parish of Raffan, Banffshire, was born 2 September and baptised in Dundee on 14 September 1811. [St Paul's Episcopal Cathedral baptismal register]

KNOPP, Captain NICHOLAS, born in Bremen, Germany, and Janet Anderson in Dundee, were married on 25 November 1810 in Dundee. [St Paul's Episcopal Cathedral marriage register]

KNOX, FRANCIS ARTHUR SKENE, an Infantry Lieutenant of the Mecklenburg Army, heir to Harriet Knox, daughter of Captain David Knox, Royal Navy, who died on 31 July 1861, re property in George Street, Edinburgh, 4 March 1869. [NRS.S/H]

KNOX, THOMAS, from Renfrew (?), a student at the University of Heidelberg, matriculated on 23 September 1615. [SIG#314][SHR.V.67][RCPE]

KOBEL, GEORGE, a painter in Munich, 1854. [NRS.NRAS.3250/46]

KOHTE, JACOB, master of the <u>Jacob</u> of <u>Bremen,</u> was admitted as a burgess and guilds-brother of Glasgow on 17 May 1716. [GBR]

KOOP, PETER, a merchant in Hamburg, a bond, 1682. [NRS.RD2.58.334]

KRAMER, KARL, born in 1833 in Germany, a street musician in Edinburgh by 1851. [Census]

KRAMER, MARY ANN, born 1830 in Germany, an assistant dress-maker in Edinburgh by 1851. [Census]

KREUTZER, BERNARD, born 1806 in Prussia, Director of Music to the Grand Duke of Baden, in Edinburgh 1851. [Census]

KREUTZER, FANNY H., born 1817 in Switzerland, a nursery maid in Edinburgh by 1851. [Census]

KRUIT, ABRAHAM, 1700. [NRS.RD2.84.487]

KRUMBEIN, HEINRICH, a music master in Edinburgh, 1707. [NRS.AC8.92]

KUHEL, CATHERINE, born 1831 in Germany, a street musician in Edinburgh by 1851. [Census]

LAMB, WILLIAM, of Aberton, settled in Elbing, father of William who was born there on 7 December 1586. [SIG#53]

LAMONT, JOHN, [Johann von Lamont], born in Braemar on 13 December 1805, educated at the Ratisbon Seminary in 1817, later the Astronomer Royal in Munich, died 1879. [SIG#295] [RSC#I.255]

LANDELS, THOMAS, from Glasgow, a student at the University of Heidelberg, matriculated on 23 December 1596. [SIG#314][SHR.V.67][RCPE]

LATTO, DAVID, born 1838, from Pittenweem, Fife, master of the <u>Persian,</u> died in Kranken Anstalt, Bremen, on 16 August 1880. [EFR:20.8.1880]

LAUDENBERG, GEORGE, stocking weaver in Elbing, Wurtemburg, 1746, referred to in a case before the High Court of the Admiralty of Scotland relating to the Palatine emigration to Pennsylvania. [NRS.AC10.317/318]

LAWSON, DAVID, son of John Lawson a merchant in Dundee, a traveller in Naumsburg, Prussia, Dundee birth brief dated 22 August 1616. [Dundee Burgh Archives]

LAWTON, RICHARD, married Sarah Metcaulf in the English Church of Hamburg on 27 May 1651. [TKH]

LEARMONTH, DAVID, was admitted as a burgess of Frankfurt-am-Main in 1471. [Frankfurt-am-Main Burgerbuch, iv, fo.340r]

LEARMONTH, G., a Captain of the Swedish Army in Germany during the 1630s, died at Boitzenburg. [SIG#283]

LEARMONTH, JOHN, a chapman, son of William Learmonth in Kelso, a prisoner in Canongate tolbooth, was released to go as a soldier under Colonel Sinclair to fight in Germany, in June 1628. [RPCS.II.333]

LEENDERS, PETER, born in Koln, a merchant in Copenhagen, husband of Hermina von Brusberg also born in Koln, 1672. [NRS.AC7.3.198]

LEGGE, WILLIAM, a Major General of the Swedish Army in Germany during the 130s; Governor of Bremen, 1633. [MGIF.Map 3][SIG#283]

LEHSTEN, AUGUST, a sea-captain from Wismar, drowned at Leith on 9 July 1883. [Leith MI]

LEISVELT, JERONIMUS, [alias Jeremy Leechfield], a

merchant from Aachen who settled in Edinburgh, traded from Leith to Guinea before 1638, a member of the Scottish Guinea Company. [SHR]

LEITH, GEORGE, at the Ratisbon Seminary in 1718. [SIG#294][RSC#I.250]

LEITH, JAMES, son of James Leith and his wife Jelis at the Kirk of Crathie, Aberdeenshire, settled in Prussia, 1586. [APB]

LEITH, ROBERT, at the Ratisbon Seminary in 1718. [SIG#294]

LEITH, ….., son of Alexander Leith in Collithy, was admitted to the Monastery of Ratisbon on 29 September 1726. [SIG#294]

LENNOX, GEORGE HENRY, in Hameln, a letter, 1757. [NRS.RH4.195.3.5]

LEO, L., born 1745 in Berlin, Prussia, a dentist, landed in Harwich, settled in Edinburgh before 1803. [ECA.SL115.2.2/14]

LERMONT, Captain DAVID, was commissioned by Ernest, Prince and Count of Mansfelt, to negotiate with those who were raising Scottish regiments for service under the King and Queen of Bohemia, at Lauenburg on 24 January 1626. [NRS.GD84.Sec.2/148]

LESLIE, A., in Hamburg, 1632. [NRS.GD406.1.277]

LESLIE, ALEXANDER, Governor of Stralsund, 1629-1630, then of Frankfurt, 1631. [MGIF.Map 3][SIG#282]

LESLIE, Major General Sir ALEXANDER, of Balgonie, in Lower Saxony, a letter, 1635. [NRS.GD26.3.215]

LESLIE, ANDREW, educated at the Braunsberg Seminary around 1613, later in Rome, then a priest in Scotland. [SIG#299]

LESLIE, BONIFACE, son of Alexander Leslie of Pitcapple, was admitted to the Monastery of Ratisbon on 30 November 1709. [SIG#293]

LESLIE, ERNEST, born 1776, son of John Leslie of Balquhain, was at Ratisbon Seminary in 1788. [SIG#295][RSC#I.254]; cf Ernest Leslie of Balquhain, died in Frankfurt am Main on 15 March 1836. [AJ#4603]

LESLIE, GEORGE, a Colonel in Swedish service in Germany during 1636, then Governor of Vechta in Oldenburg, died in 1638. [SIG#283][NRS.RH15.16.22]

LESLIE, GEORGE, son of Andrew Leslie of Logiedurno, Aberdeenshire, and his wife Isabel Stewart, Adjutant General of His Imperial Majesty's Army, issued with a birth brief in 1661. [APB]

LESLIE, JAMES, educated at the Braunsberg Seminary around 1608, became a Jesuit. [SIG#299]

LESLIE, JOHN, educated at the Braunsberg Seminary around 1613, later in Rome. [SIG#299]

LESLIE, JOHN, a Major General of the Swedish Army in Germany during the 1630s; Governor of Frankfurt, 1631. [MGIF.Map 3][SIG#283]

LESLIE, JOHN, a rebel imprisoned in Perth who was released to go to Germany in 1691. [RPCS.XVI.264]

LESLIE, JOHN, at the Ratisbon Seminary in 1713, died 1779. [SIG#294][RSC#I.250]

LESLIE, JOHN, born 1781, son of John Leslie of Balquhain, was at Ratisbon Seminary in 1788. [SIG#295][RSC#I.254]

LESLIE, LUDOVICK, a Colonel of the Swedish Army in Germany during the 1630s. [SIG#283]

LESLIE, NORMAND, son of John Leslie, a portioner of
Buchanstane, and his wife Constance, a traveller in
Pomerania and Prussia, 1591. [APB]

LESLIE, ROBERT, son of Robert Leslie portioner of
Logiedurno, Aberdeenshire, and his wife Isobel Stewart,
Adjutant General to His Imperial Majesty's Army before
1661. [APB]

LESLIE, Sir WALTER, son of John Leslie of Balqhan and his
wife Jean Erskine, a Colonel in Hungary by 1637.
[RGS.IX.648]

LESLIE, Count, in Graz, letter, 1691. [NRS.GD406.1.3730]

LEVIN, GUMFRIG, born 1744 in Ragusen, Prussia, then in
Gothenburg, Sweden, arrived at Bo'ness during November
1804, residing at Grassmarket, Edinburgh, in January 1806.
[ECA.SL115.2.2/50]

LEYENDECKER, JOHN, a merchant in Aachen, 1701.
[NRS.RD3.98.294]

LIBENEN, MATHIAS, master of the St Mary of Lubeck, April
1628. [NRS.AC7.1]

LIDDEL, DUNCAN, born 1561, son of John Liddel a burgess of
Aberdeen, educated at King's College, Aberdeen, emigrated
to Danzig in 1579, a student at Frankfurt-on-the Oder in
1576, a physician and scholar at the University of Helmstadt
in 1591, died in Aberdeen on 17 December 1613.
[SIG#313][St Nicholas gravestone, Aberdeen]

LIEBIG, Dr JUSTUS, Professor of Chemistry of the University
if Giessen, was admitted as an honorary burgess of Glasgow
on 10 October 1844. [GBR]

LILBURN, HENRY, a cleric of the Diocese of Aberdeen,
matriculated at the University of Koln in 1443.
[SNQ.X.3/77]

LINCZOW (?), ANDREW, a quartermaster in the service of the Elector of Brandenburg around 1660. [NRS.GD10/531]

LINDSAY, ALEXANDER, a Colonel of the Swedish Army in Germany during the 1630s. [SIG#283]

LINDSAY, DAVID, a student at Frankfurt-on-the Oder in 1656. [SIG#313]

LINDSAY, G., a Colonel of the Swedish Army in Germany during the 1630s. [SIG#283]

LINDSAY, Colonel HENRY, at Lutze, 1638. [STAUL.HL#685]; a Colonel of the Swedish Army in Germany during the 1630s, died in Hamburg. [SIG#283]

LINDSAY, JAMES, educated at the Braunsberg Seminary around 1596, a Jesuit who died in Scotland during 1624. [SIG#299]

LINDSAY, J., a Colonel of the Swedish Army in Germany during the 1630s, died at Neumark. [SIG#283]

LINDSAY, PATRICK, a student at the University of Heidelberg, matriculated on 21 January 1603. [SIG#314][SHR.V.67][RCPE]

LINNEN, MATHIAS, [alias Matthew Lynnen], a merchant from Aachen who settled in Edinburgh, traded from Leith to Guinea before 1638, a member of the Scottish Guinea Company. [SHR]

LIPMAN, ISAAC, and his wife Ida Rothschild, had their daughters Cecilia and Bertha baptised in Dundee on 1 March 1849 and 11 February 1851 respectively. [Dundee Baptismal Register]

LISTER, GEORGE, a student at the University of Helmstadt in 1593. [SIG#313]

LITTERBROODT, JOOST, a merchant in Hamburg, 1676.
[NRS.AC7.4]

LITTLE, JOHN, from Edinburgh, a student of theology, died in
Geneva during 1622, autopsy and certificate.
[NRS.GD122.15.14/15]

LIVINGSTONE, JAMES, in Heidelberg, 1614.
[NRS.RH15/11/2]

LIVINGSTONE, JOHN, (Hans Leveston), member of the
Scottish Brotherhood at Greifswald, around 1600.
[SIG#315]

LOCKHART, JAMES, of Carnwath, was granted the title of
Baron, by Maria Theresa, Empress of Germany, in Vienna
on 24 April 1762. [NRS.Lyon Office, GI.148];
Commissioned in the service of the Empress Maria Theresa
and Joseph II, Emperor of Germany, 1768. [NRS.GD2.60-
61]

LOHE, ADOLPHUS, a merchant who was admitted as a burgess
and guilds-brother of Edinburgh on 19 May 1708. [EBR]

LOSCH, KARL, from Fockenburg, Limbach, died in Dundee
during 1861. [NRS.NRAS.3250/52]

LOTHIAN, HENRY, ["Heinrich Laudien"], and his wife
Elizabeth, from Edinburgh, a trader in Elbing, East Prussia,
1606.

LOTHIAN, PETER, ["Peter Laudien"], born in Edinburgh
around 1580, died in Danzig on 13 December 1635,
husband of Christina Muttray from Aberdeen.

LOTHIAN, THOMAS, ["Thomas Laudien"], a mariner from
Edinburgh, was admitted as a citizen of Danzig 27 March
1624.

LOW, Major GEORGE, settled in Bremen, died there 1699.

[NRS.RH15.106.532/8]

LOW, HENRY, son of John Low and his wife Margaret Mealling in Coulinns, Drumoak, settled in Prussia, 1584. [APB]

LOW, JAMES, born 1838, son of James Low and his wife Jean Smith, died in Hamburg on 25 August 1857. [Barry, Angus, gravestone]

LOW, WILLIAM, a student at the University of Rostock in 1580. [SIG#313]

LOWSON, ANDREW, a student at Frankfurt-on-the-Oder, 1549. [SIG#313]

LUDEMAN, HANS, master of the White Unicorn of Hamburg, 1627. [NRS.AC7.1.60]

LUMSDEN, ALEXANDER, a student at the Scots College in Douai around 1641, at Wurzburg from 1644 to 1645, at the Scots College in Rome in 1645. [SF#275]

LUMSDEN, Sir JAMES, of Invergellie, a Lieutenant Colonel in Germany, husband of Christian Rutherford, 1635. [NRS.RSXI.273]; Governor of Osnabruck, 1633-1639. [MGIF.Map 3]; a Colonel of the Swedish Army in Germany during the 1630s. [SIG#283]

LUMSDEN, JANET HILL, born 1861, daughter of F. R. Lumsden, parish schoolmaster at Wood's School, Newburn, Fife, and his wife Janet W. Hill, died in Treves, Rhenish Prussia, on 30 April 1879. [Fife Herald: 8.5.1879] [S#11,167]

LUMSDEN,........., a Colonel of the Swedish Army in Germany during the 1630s. [SIG#283]

LUNDIE, Lieutenant Colonel JAMES, commander of Bremervorde, 1649 to 1657. [MGIF.73; map 3]

LUNDIE, ROBERT A., MA, MB, Edinburgh, married Annie, youngest daughter of Charles Henry Moore, Honorable East India Company Service, at the British Legation, Stuttgart, on 8 August 1884. [EC#31168]

LUTMAN, JEREMIAH, a servant to the Duke of Argyll, was admitted as a burgess of Glasgow on 6 January 1716. [GBR]

LYELL, MATILDA, born 1843, daughter of James Lyall and Margaret Simpson, died in Heidelber on 18 January 1862. [Pert, Angus, gravestone]

LYON, HERMAN, born 1748 in Moghedorf, Germany, later a dentist in Prisel in Brabant, settled in the Linenhall, Canongate, Edinburgh, by 1798. [ECA.SL115.2.1/71]

LYON, Major JOHN, a soldier who returned to Scotland from Germany in 1650. [RPCS.XVI.526]

MACALL, ADAM, from Edinburgh, admitted to the Monastery of Ratisbon on 13 July 1597. [SIG#292]

MACCOLL, DONALD, born in Achagphouple, near Fort William, in 1835, at the Ratisbon Seminary in 1855, was ordained as a priest. [SIG#296][RSC#I.259]

MACDONALD, ALEXANDER, ordained as a Catholic priest at Douai in 1775, priest in Uist until 1781, a monk at Wurtzburg from 1785 until his death on 2 January 1810. [IR.XVIII.152]

MACDONALD, ALLAN, born 21 July 1825, was at the Ratisbon Seminary in 1838, died 2 April 1840. [SIG#295] [RSC.#I.256]

MACDONALD, ANGUS, born 1779, was at Ratisbon Seminary in 1791-92. [SIG#295][RSC#I.254]

MACDONALD, ANGUS, born 25 September 1818, was at the

Ratisbon Seminary in 1830, died on 19 March 1843.
[SIG#295][RSC#I.255]

MACDONALD, ARCHIBALD, born in Glenuig, Moydart, on 9
November 1828, was\educated at Ratisbon Seminary from
1841 to 1845, returned to Scotland. [RSC#I.257]

MACDONALD, COLL, born in Inch, Lochaber, on 6 January
1832, was at the Ratisbon Seminary from 1841 to 1845,
returned to Scotland. [SIG#296][RSC#I.257]

MACDONALD, DAVID, born in Fort William, Inverness-shire,
on 6 March 1832, was at the Ratisbon Seminary from 1841
to 1845. [SIG#296][RSC#I.257]

MCDONALD, Sir JAMES, in Lausanne, probate 13 August
1832, Prob.11/1304 PCC

MACDONALD, JOHN, born 2 July 1818, was at the Ratisbon
Seminary in 1830, a priest in Eskdale by 1862, then a
bishop 24 February 1869. [SIG#295][RSC#I.255]

MACDONALD, JOHN, born in Glasgow on 12 April 1837, was
at the Ratisbon Seminary in 1852. [SIG#296] [RSC#I.258]

MACDONALD, MAURICE, from the Hebrides, a monk at the
Scots Monastery at Wurzburg in 1791. [SOG#304]

MACDONEL, ALEXANDER, was at Ratisbon Seminary in
1764. [SIG#295][RSC#I.253]

MACDONEL, CHARLES, was at Ratisbon Seminary in 1764.
[SIG#295][RSC#I.253]

MACDONEL, JOHN, at the Ratisbon Seminary in 1719.
[SIG#294]

MACDONEL, JOHN, at the Ratisbon Seminary in 1735.
[RSC#I.251]

MACDONEL, JOHN, was at Ratisbon Seminary in 1756. [SIG#295][RSC#I.252]

MACDONEL, WILLIAM, was admitted to the Monastery of Ratisbon on 29 September 1726. [SIG#294]

MACDOUGAL, JAMES, Governor of Stralsund, 1630, then of Frankfurt, 1631. [MGIF.Map 3]; a Colonel of the Swedish Army in Germany during the 1630s. "he stormed Landsberg, defended Schweinfurt, and beat the Imperial troops at Liegnitz". [SIG#283]

MCDOUGAL, TOBIAS, Governor of Gardelegen, 1642-1648. [MGIF.Map 3]

MCDOUGALL, ..., commander of Brandenburg troops, 1633. [NRS.GD246.26.5.21]

MCEWAN, MARY, eldest daughter of the late James McEwan, South Lodge, Stirling, married Louis Wilhelm Bode, a Lieutenant of the Royal Hanoverian Leib regiment, at the British Consulate in Cologne, and later at the English Chapel of the Prince of Prussia in Koblenz on 4 January 1858. [W.XIX.1941]

MCEWAN, WILHELMINA SHIREFF, third daughter of the late James McEwan, South Lodge, Stirling, married Theodore Louis Von Klenck late of the Royal Hanoverian Leib regiment, at the British Consulate in Cologne, and later at the English Chapel of the Prince of Prussia in Koblenz on 20 May 1858. [W.XIX.1980]

MCGAW, RICHARD B., in Hamburg, son of Richard McGaw (1780-1867) and Agnes McMurtrie (1795-1873). [Barr gravestone]

MCGOUN, DUNCAN MALCOLM, a merchant in Hamburg, son of Janet Stewart or McGoun in Greenock, 1844. [NRS.S/H]

MACGOWAN, JOHN, born in Glasgow on 13 November 1841, was at the Ratisbon Seminary in 1852, died in 1861. [SIG#296][RSC#I.258]

MACGREGOR, CALUM, at the Ratisbon Seminary in 1719. [SIG#294][RSC#I.251]

MACINNES, JOHN, born in Linwood, parish of Kilbarchan, Renfrewshire, on 16 July 1833, at Ratisbon Seminary in 1855, ordained as a priest in 1862, returned to Scotlaand and in 1875 was sent to Canada. [SIG#296][RSC#I.259]

MCINTOSH, AENEAS, of Raigmore, born 1741, a Lieutenant of Keith's Highlanders in Germany until 1763, died 1786, husband of Ann McPherson 1747 to 1837. [Moy gravestone]

MACINTOSH, DONALD, born in Glenfinnan, educated at the Ratisbon Seminary in 1855, ordained as a priest and sent to Scotland on a mission in 1862. [SIG#1855][RSC#I.259]

MACINTOSH, DONALD, born 1732, matriculated at the Ratisbon Seminary in 1739. [SIG#294][RSC#I.252]

MCINTOSH, MICHAEL, a priest at the Monastery of St James, Wurzburg, dead by 1670. [SF#280]

MCINTOSH, WILLIAM, in Eisenbach and Dutchey, probate 13 April 1816. [NA.Prob.11/1579]

MACIVER, ARCHIBALD AUGUSTIN, born on 31 December 1780, was at Ratisbon Seminary in 1791-92, Dean of St James in Regensburg, 1832, died as Dean of the Cathedral at Ratisbon. [SIG#295][RSC#I.254][NRS.NRAS.3250/24]

MCKAY, Mrs AUGUSTE L. E., in Switzerland, 1866. [NRS.RD5.1257/556]

MCKAY, Sir DONALD, of Strathnaver, was appointed Colonel of a regiment of 3000 Scots raised for service in Bohemia and who were to be shipped to Gluckstadt, 4 March 1626. [NRS.GD84, Sec.2/149]; a Colonel of the Swedish Army in Germany during 1630s. [SIG#283]

MACKAY, JACOB, a small trader in Wismar around 1579 to 1592. [SIG#51]

MACKAY, W., a Captain of the Swedish Army in Germany during the 1630s, died at Lutzen. [SIG#283]

MACKAY, ..., a Captain of the Swedish Army in Germany during the 1630s. [SIG#283]

MCKENZIE, Reverend GEORGE, in Frankfurt, 1875. [NRS.RD5.1570.209]

MCKENZIE, ISOBEL, daughter of Hector McKenzie late of the Hudson Bay Company, died in Davos Platz, Switzerland, on 20 January 1880. [EC#29744]

MCKERRALL, ROBERT, died in Frankfort on 25 April 1841. [W.II.140]

MACKIE, BONIFACE, born around 1658, to Wurzburg in 1677, ordained in December 1682, died in Edinburgh 1712. [SF#281]

MACLEAN, ANDREW, matriculated at Wurzburg on 12 June 1625, studied physics. [SF#272]

MACLEAN, PETER, Governor of Stralsund, 1679-1697. [MGIF.Map 3]

MACLEAN, ROBERT, born 1604 in Dumfries, a student at the Scots College in Douai around 1621, and by 1623 in Wurzburg, dead by September 1628. [SF#274-279]

MACLENNAN, CALUM, from Stornaway, the Diocese of Sodor, was admitted to the Monastery of Ratisbon on 2 February 1689. [SIG#293]; matriculated at Wurzburg on 6

November 1694, studied theology. [SF#272]

MACLENNAN, RODERICK, from Kintail, a student at the University of Heidelberg, matriculated 30 April 1660. [SIG#314][SHR.V.67][RCPE]

MACNAUGHTON, JAMES, born 8 March 1802, was at the Ratisbon Seminary in 1817, died in America during 1862. [SIG#295] [RSC#I.255]

MACNAVISH, ARCHIBALD, from Moydart, was at the Ratisbon Seminary in 1841. [SIG#296]

MCNEILL, BEATRICE, third daughter of the late Forbes McNeill and niece of Lord Colonsay of Colonsay and of Sir John McNeill, married Henry Lorenz, eldest son of C. F. Lorenz of Hamburg, in Brixton on 23 January 1859. [W.XX.2063]

MACPHERSON, ROBERT, born 1780, was at Ratisbon Seminary in 1791-92. [SIG#295][RSC#I.254]

MACRAE, ALEXANDER, born in Mulardich, Strathglass, on 12 September 1829, was at the Ratisbon Seminary in 1841, returned to Scotland, died at Blairs College. [SIG#295] [RSC#I.257]

MACREDIE, ROBERT REID, died in Stuttgart, Wurtemburg, on 10 February 1859. [W.XX.2059]

MACSWAIN, HUGH, born 27 December 1820, was at the Ratisbon Seminary in 1838, returned to Scotland and became a schoolmaster, by 1855 he was a novice with the Passionists in England. [SIG#295][RSC#I.256]

MAHLSTEDT, or SCHMIDT, MARION, wife of Luder Mahlstedt, farmer, Hagen, Hanover, was served as heir to her mother Jane Irving or Schmidt, wife of Arp. Schmidt in Stellerbruch near Bremen who died on 29 October 1831, re a house near the Figgate Burn in Edinburgh, 28 December

1849. [NRS.S/H]

MAITLAND, STUART CAIRNS, of Dundrennan, died in Dresden on 4 December 1861. [W#XXII.2364]

MAK, JOHN, a merchant in Hamburg, 1675. [NRS.RD3.40.32]

MALCOLM, JOHN, son of James Malcolm and his wife Elspet Ranzie in Bowhill, Banchory, Aberdeenshire, a traveller in Prussia before 1596. [APB]

MALCOLM, WILLIAM ALEXANDER, a gentleman in Cologne, probate 22 July 1835 PCC. [NA.Prob.11/1849]

MANSA, JOHN JAMES, pastor of the Reformed Church at NRSsau Saarbrocke, petition for aid, 1761. [NRS.CH1/2/102/fos.184-191]

MARIGNAC, PETER, from Geneva, a medical graduate of Edinburgh University in 1805. [EMG#39]

MARJORYBANKS, MARION ANNIE, daughter of Edward Marjorybanks, married Colonel Richard von Westerhagen, in St Peter's, Heidelberg, on 2 August 1884. [EC#31167]

MARTINER, JOSEPH, born 1780 in the Tirol, emigrated from Hamburg to Leith, residing in Canongate, Edinburgh, by 1801. [ECA.SL115.2.1/133]

MARSHALL, ALEXANDER, son of John Mitchell and his wife Helen Irving in Arbedie, a traveller in Pomerania, 1599. [APB]

MARSHALL, ROBERT, son of John Mitchell and his wife Helen Irving in Arbedie, a traveller in Pomerania, 1599. [APB]

MARTINE, JOHN GODARD, of Hamburg, was admitted as a honorary burgess and guilds-brother of Glasgow on 21 January 1779. [Glasgow Burgess Roll]

MASSON, JAMES, at the Ratisbon Seminary in 1713.
[SIG#294][RSC#I.250]

MATHER, ARCHIBALD, son of James Mather and his wife
Christine Melville, died in Hamburg on 10 March 1850.
[Ferry Port on Craig MI]

MATHIE, JOHN, in Bremen, master of the Jenny Crawford,
letters, 1740-1741. [NRS.RH15.38.91/92]

MAXWELL, BERNARD, born 1641, Abbot of Wurzburg in
1679-1685, died 17 March 1685. [SF#272-280]

MAXWELL, EDWARD, born around 1607 in Conheath near
Dumfries, a student at the Scots College in Douai around
1621, and by May 1623 in Wurzburg, dead by October
1635. [SF#274-279]

MAXWELL, WILLIAM, professed in the Monastery of St
James, Wurzburg before 1631, in Ireland in September
1635. [SF#279]

MAXWELL, ..., son of Lieutenant Colonel C. F. Maxwell,
was born in Wiesbaden on 20 February 1856.
[W.XVII.1738]

MAYNE, JOHN, born 1583 in Glasgow, a student at the Scots
College in Rome around 1619, then a monk in Wurzburg,
administrator of Ratisbon from 1636 to 1639, died there in
October 1639. [SF#275, 279]

MEARNS, GRACE, a widow in Bonn on the Lower Rhine, 25
July 1850. [NRS.B22.4.60.148]

MELDRUM, JOHN, soldier in Hamburg, 1630. [SSNE#572]

MELDRUM, THOMAS, in Hamburg, 1623

MELVILLE, Colonel ANDREW, commandant of Gifhorn from
1677 to 1680. [MAM.214][MGIF.Map 3]

MELVILLE, DAVID, 3rd Earl of Leven, in Berlin, 1697.
[NRS.GD1.832.5]

MELVILLE, THOMAS, graduated MA from Glasgow
University in 1747, an experimental philosopher, died in
Geneva during December 1753. [RGG]

MELVIN, RICHARD, a student at the University of Greifswald,
1546. [SIG#314]

MELVIN, THOMAS, from Dysart, Fife, matriculated at the
University of Heidelberg on 25 November 1613.
[SHR.V.67][RCPE]

MENTEITH, JOHN, matriculated at Heidelberg University on
15 March 1568. [SHR.V.67][SIG#314]

MENZIES, ALEXANDER, educated at the Braunsberg
Seminary around 1641, died in Braunsberg during 1671.
[SIG#299]

MENZIES, ALEXANDER, son of the laird of Pitfoddels, at the
Ratisbon Seminary in 1719. [SIG#294]

MENZIES, ALEXANDER, born on 6 December 1723, brother
of the laird of Pitfoddels, matriculated at the Ratisbon
Seminary in 1735. [RSC#I.251]

MENZIES, DAVID, son of the laird of Pitfoddels, at the Ratisbon
Seminary in 1719. [SIG#294]

MENZIES, DAVID, born 15 August 1722, entered the Ratisbon
Seminary in 1735. [RSC.I.251]

MENZIES, JAMES, at the Ratisbon Seminary in 1719.
[SIG#294]

MENZIES, JAMES, entered to Ratisbon Seminary in 1735.
[RSC#I.251]

MENZIES, JOHN, was admitted to the Monastery of Ratisbon in 1742. [SIG#294]

MENZIES, WILLIAM, educated at the Braunsberg Seminary around 1641. [SIG#299]

MENZIES, WILLIAM, son of the laird of Pitfoddels, at the Ratisbon Seminary in 1719. [SIG#294]

MENZIES, WILLIAM, born on 25 May 1721, matriculated at the Ratisbon Seminary in 1735. [RSC#I.251]

MEYER, ELIZABETH, born 1802 in Switzerland, a lady's maid in Edinburgh by 1851. [Census]

MEYER, JOHN, son of Arnold Meyer, in Bremen, a deed, 1702. [NRS.RD2.86.1.631]

MEYER, OTTO, a merchant from Hamburg, in the Shetland Islands, 1653.

MEYER, THEODORE T., born 1818 in Germany, a teacher of Hebrew and German in Edinburgh by 1851. [Census]

MILL, WILLIAM, son of Andrew Mill and his wife Margaret in Newton of Troine, Aberchirder, Banffshire, settled in Neustayn, Pomerania, 1595. [APB]

MILLER, JOHN, son of William Miller in Jedburgh, a prisoner in Edinburgh tolbooth, was released to go as a soldier under Colonel Sinclair to fight in Germany, in June 1628. [RPCS.II.333]

MILLER, JOHN, born in Edinburgh, was at the Ratisbon Seminary in 1852. [SIG#295][RSC#I.257]

MITCHELL, Sir ANDREW, born on 15 April 1708 in Edinburgh, was appointed as Ambassador to Prussia in 1756, died on 28 January 1771. [SIG#206-210]

MITCHELL, ANDREW, of Thainstoun, British Ambassador in Berlin, 1729-1772, papers; in Leipzig, a letter, 1761. [NRS.RH4.70; GD248.183.4]

MITCHELL, DUNCAN, in Heidelberg, 1852. [NRS.RD5.911/401]

MITCHELL, GEORGE JOSEPH, born 9 August 1831 in Aberdeen, was educated at the Ratisbon Seminary from 1845 to 1848. [RSC#I.257]

MITCHELL, JOHN, in Edinburgh, formerly in Hamburg, 1821-1824. [NRS.CS46/1841, 4726]

MITCHELL, JOSEPH, from Aberdeen, was at the Ratisbon Seminary in 1845. [SIG#295]

MITCHELL, MARY, born 1780 in Germany, settled in Edinburgh by 1851. [Census]

MOIR, JAMES, born 20 December 1761, was at Ratisbon Seminary in 1772. [SIG#295][RSC#I.253]

MOIR, Reverend JAMES, in Ratisbon, heir to his father John Moir in Peterhead, Aberdeenshire, formerly in Kirkton of Longside, 30 July 1828. [NRS.S/H]

MOIR, THOMAS, was at Ratisbon Seminary in 1784. [SIG#295][RSC#I.254]

MOLLISON, Colonel JOHN, Governor of Lunenburg, applied for, and was given, a birth-brief from the Privy Council of Scotland in 1674. [RPCS.IV.185][MAM.153][MGIF.Map 3]

MONCREIFF, ..., a Captain of the Swedish Army in Germany during the 1630s, died at Brandenburg. [SIG#283]

MONRO, JOHN, born 1830, son of Arthur Monro and his wife Helen Reid, died in Hamburg on 5 December 1859.

[Rosyth, Fife, MI]

MONTGOMERY, DUNCAN, in Hamburg, probate 24 March 1806 PCC. [NA.Prob.11/1440]

MONTGOMERY, THOMAS, a student at the University of Rostock in 1592. [SIG#313]

MORE, HENRY, was educated at the Scots College in Rome from 1633 to 1639, later a Benedictine in Germany. [SF#275]

MORE, Major PATRICK, commandant of Buxtehude, near Hamburg, 1646 to 1670s. [MGIF.221; map 3]

MORE, PATRICK, in Oldenburg and Bremen around 1664, [NRS.NRAS#2838/bundle 424]; and his wife Margaretha, possibly from Perth, in Buxtenhude, Duchy of Bremen, 1682. [NRS.B59.24.12.3]

MORISON, AUGUSTUS, from the Diocese of Aberdeen, was admitted to the Monastery of Ratisbon on 25 February 1704, died 1734. [SIG#293]

MORTAN, DAVID, in Anklam, near Greifswald, 1606-1612. **[HKA]**

MOWBRAY, R., in Hamburg, 1796. [NRS.NRAS#3955/60/2/192]

MOWER, MARTIN, master of the St Laurence of Lubeck, 1627. [NRS.AC7.2.117]

MOWK, CORTE, master of the St Peter of Lubeck, 1628. [NRS.AC7.1.160]

MUNRO, Sir HECTOR, of Foulis, of the Swedish Army in Germany during the 1630s, died at Buxtehude. [SIG#283]; died in Hamburg, 1635. [WMF.57-59]

MUNRO, ROBERT, of Foulis, a Colonel in Swedish service, died at Ulm, Wurtemberg, on 29 April 1633, buried in the Franciscan church in Ulm. [Ulm town council book] [SIG#283]

MURDISON, JOHN, "Joannes Murdisinus", a student at the University of Helmstadt in 1588. [SIG#313]

MURDOCH, Mrs ANNA WALLACE, relict of George Wallace in New South Wales, died in Homburg near Frankfort on 29 July 1852. [W.XIII.1354]

MURE, JAMES, in Gottingen, 1818. [NRS.GD35/144]

MURRAY, ANGUS, ("Enghus Murre"), member of the Shetland Company in Hamburg, around 1593. [SAH/VDHS]

MURRAY, JAMES, married Margaret Davidson in the English Church of Hamburg on 3 January 1626. [TKH]

MURRAY, JAMES, born 19 March 1734, second son of Lord George Murray and his wife Amelia, a Lieutenant of the Saxon Grenadier Guards from 1751-1756. [SP]

MURRAY, JOHN, ["Goen Murre"], member of the Shetland Company in Hamburg, around 1620. [SAH/VDHS]

MURRAY, JOHN, ["Hans Morrha"], a Scot, married Alheitd, a widow, in St Jacobi church, Hamburg, 1707. [TKH]

MURRAY, JOHN, in Gottingen, 1751. [NRS.NRAS#234/box 45a/2/2/40]

MURRAY, JOHN ROSS, Captain of Keith's Highlanders, in Warburg, 1760. [NRS.NRAS#234/box 47/12/122]

MURRAY, THOMAS, a student at the University of Heidelberg, 1593, matriculated on 22 February 1593. [SIG#314][SHR.V.67][RCPE]

MURRAY, THOMAS, member of the Scottish Brotherhood at Greifswald, around 1600. [SIG#315]

MURRAY, VIRGINIA MARY, Convent of St Anne in Munich, 1847. [NRS.NRAS.3250/22]

MUSTARD, ALEXANDER, a student at the University of Greifswald, 1545. [SIG#314]

NAIRN, DAVID, from St Andrews, a student at the University of Heidelberg, matriculated on 31 July 1609. [SIG#314][SHR.V.67][RCPE]

NAIRN, JOHN, Governor of Erfurt, 1640s, and of Leipzig, 1648-1649. [MGIF.Map 3]

NEISS, JOACHIM, a merchant in Wismar, 1677. [NRS.AC7.4]

NEITHARDT, ..., son of Louis Neithardt, was born in Dresden on 20 January 1880. [EC#29744]

NELSON, EDWARD, born 1815 in Annan, Dumfries-shire, son of Benjamin Nelson and his wife Christian Irving Forrest, MD, died in Heidelberg on 21 April 1837. [Annan gravestone]

NICOLSON, ARTHUR, a merchant from Lerwick, Shetland Islands, in Hamburg by 1702. [NRS.RH15.93.52; RH15.93.16.15/16]

NOEHDEN, GEORGE HEINRICH, born in Gottingen on 23 January 1770, graduated LL.D. from Glasgow University in 1812, died on 14 March 1826. [RGG]

OGILVIE, GEORGE, settled in Germany during the Thirty Years War and became Commandant of the fortress of Spielberg, near Brunn in Moravia. [SIG#316]

OGILVIE, Sir GEORGE, a Colonel in the Army of the Emperor, son of Sir Patrick Ogilvie of Muirton in Angus, genealogy,

29 March 1723. [NRS.Lyon Office. 28-31]

OGILVIE, ISIDORE, born 1670, matriculated at Wurzburg in 1693, ordained in 1694, died in April 1701. [SF#272/281]

OGILVIE, JOHN, a student at the Scots College in Douai around 1596, and by 1598 was a monk at Ratisbon. [SF#274]

OGILVIE, THOMAS JOSEPH, a lay-brother in the MoNRStary of Wurzburg in 1684. [SF#281]

OGILVIE, WILLIAM, matriculated at Wurzburg on 11 August 1628, Abbot of Wurzburg 1615-1635, died 17 September 1635. [SF#272/279]

OLDERMANN, JOHN, LL.D., Hamburg, died 17 February 1841, inventory, 1846, Comm. Edinburgh. [NRS]

OSTEN, Baron WILLIAM, a general in Hanoverian service, died 24 January 1852, inventory, 1852, Comm. Edinburgh. [NRS]

OTTE, JAMES, partner of the Nightingale of Bremen, deeds, 1673. [NRS.RD3.33.721/724]

OTTERBEG, or HECKLEBECK, INGLEBERT, a jeweller and goldsmith, burgess of the Canongate, Edinburgh, 1643. [OEC.19.14]

OTTINGAR, CONRAD, a goldsmith in the Canongate, Edinburgh, 1648. [OEC.19.16]

PANISCIM, BRODER, master of the St John of Frederickstadt, 1668. [NRS.RD4.20.578]

PANTON, JEREMY, from Aberdeen, was admitted to the Monastery of Ratisbon on 21 March 1687, died 1719. [SIG#293]

PATERSON, JOHN, a merchant in Mito, Prussia, testament confirmed with the Commissariat of Edinburgh on 27 April

1665. [NRS]

PAULSON, PAUL, a merchant in Hamburg, 1652. [NRS.GD57.336.10]

PEACOCK, ROBERT, born in Paisley, Renfrewshire, during 1796, died at his home in Lubeck on 2 March 1880. [EC#29779]

PEARSON, ALEXANDER, a student at the University of Greifswald in 1622. [SIG#314]

PEBLIS, G. J., in Heidelberg, and Zurich, 1633-1635. [NRS.GD406.1.9339-9340-9342-9371]

PEDDIE, DAVID, a student at the University of Greifswald, 1546. [SIG#314]

PENMAN, JAMES, formerly a clerk to Peter Taylor a British Army contractor in Germany, then an estate manager in East Florida around 1766, later by 1772 a merchant in St Augustine. [NRS.NRAS.771, bundle 295/491]

PEPPER, KILIAN, senior of the Scots Monastery at Wurzburg, 1820. [NRS.NRAS.3250.17/18]

PETRIE, ALEXANDER, minister of the Scots Church in Bremen, husband of Margaret Veitch, 1649. [ECA.Moses.96/4127]

PFLAUMB, CHRISTOPHER JOANNES, a German in a Dutch regiment, graduated MD from King's College, Aberdeen, on 17 August 1719. [KCA#126]

PHILLIP, WILLIAM, Governor of Demmin, 1656. [MGIF.Map 3]

PHILLIPS, ELIZABETH, born in Germany during 171793, a broom-girl of 123 Seagate, Dundee, buried there on 14 September 1833, her daughter Margaretta, born in Germany during 1826, was buried 20 September 1833, both died of cholera. [Dundee burial register]

PHILIPSON, WILLIAM, a priest of the Diocese of Aberdeen, matriculated at the University of Koln in 1512. [SNQ.X.3/78]

PIERSON, Dr JOHN EDWARD, in Berlin, genealogy, 4 October 1899. [NRS.Lyon Office. GIII.54]

PINCUS, MARTZ, born 1820 in Schwerin, Mecklenburg, a merchant in Edinburgh by 1851. [Census]

PLENDERLEITH, DAVID, a student at Frankfurt-on-the-Oder in 1699. [SIG#313]

POELLNITZ, PAULINE AMELIE, eldest daughter of Baron Frederic Poellnitz of Chateau Frankenberg, Bavaria, married George K. E. Fairholme, third son of the late George Fairholme of Greenknowe, Berwickshire, at the British Embassy in Frankfurt on 14 January 1857. [W.XVIII.1834]

POELHRITZ, Baron WALTER, of the Bavarian Army, and Mary A. Blyth, a marriage contract, 1876. [NRS.RD5.1616.87]

PONTSACK, THOMAS, a merchant in Bremen, 1730. [NRS.AC8.426]

PRINGLE, COLIN, born 1773, former Lieutenant Colonel of HM German Legion, died in Dunkirk on 7 June 1857. [W.XVIII.1880]

PURVIS, ARTHUR LAW, third son of John Purvis of Kinaldy, Fife, died in Dresden on 23 June 1872. [PJ]

RAE, JOHN, son of John Rae, a merchant in Goldape, Prussia, 1661. [NRS.RD3.3.146]

RAIT, ALEXANDER, son of Joseph Rait and his wife Jelis Strachan in Haugh of Towie, Aberdeenshire, settled in Prussia before 1590. [APB]

RAMSAY, ALEXANDER, third son of the Baron of Banff, a student at the University of Heidelberg, matriculated on 8 November 1606. [SIG#314][SHR.V.67]

RAMSAY, ALEXANDER, Major General of the Swedish Army in Germany during 1630s; Governor of Kreuznach, 1632-1633. [MGIF.Map 3][SIG#283]

RAMSAY, A., a Colonel of the Swedish Army in Germany during the 1630s. [SIG#283]

RAMSAY, Lieutenant Colonel JAMES, in Bohemia, 1620. [STW#111][MGIF.Map 3]

RAMSAY, Sir JAMES, Major General of the Swedish Army in Germany in 1630s, Governor of Hanau, 1634-1638. [STW#284][SIG#283]

RAMSAY, JAMES, Governor of Breisach, 1630. [MGIF.Map.3]

RAMSAY, JOHN, in Gilmerton, a prisoner in Canongate tolbooth, was released to go as a soldier under Colonel Sinclair to fight in Germany, in June 1628. [RPCS.II.333]

RAMSAY, General JOHN, of Kinkell, died in Geneva on 10 August 1845, inventory, 1845, Comm. Edinburgh. [NRS]

RAMSAY, WILLIAM, a graduate of St Andrews University, a student at the University of Wittenberg, 1544. [SIG#305]

RAMSAY, WILLIAM HAMILTON, Captain of the 1st Royal Lanark Militia, married Fanny Scarth, eldest daughter of Thomas Scarth, at the British Embassy in Dresden on 27 August 1857. [W.XVIII.1902]

RANDEMEDEN, DANIEL, partner of the <u>Nightingale of</u>

Bremen, a deed, 1673. [NRS.RD3.33.724]

RANKEN, JOHN, in Vienna, probate 9 July 1839, Prob.11/1914 PCC

RANSON, JACOB, master of the St Andrew of Frederickstadt, 28 August 1628. [NRS.AC7.1.175]

RAPP, CHARLES GOTTFRIED EDWARD, a merchant in Bonn, an inventory, 1874. [NRS.SC70.168.883/169.631]

RATIEN, DIEDRICH, in Bremen, 1740-1741. [NRS.RH15.38.91/92]

REID, ALEXANDER, a student at Frankfurt-on-the-Oder in 1589. [SIG#313]

REID, ALEXANDER, matriculated at the Ratisbon Seminary in 1788, died there. [RSC#I.254][SIG#295]

REID, ALEXANDER, born 15 February 1828, was at the Ratisbon Seminary in 1838, later a missionary in Scotland. [SIG#295] [RSC#I.256]

REID, EPHRAIM, from Tain, Ross-shire, was admitted to the Monastery of Ratisbon on 15 April 1663, died 1712. [SIG#293]

REID, JAMES, servant to Colonel Robert Reid, at Lutze, 1638. [STAUL.HL#685]

REID, JAMES, born 7 September 1809, was at the Ratisbon Seminary in 1817. [SIG#295] [RSC#I.255]

REID, LUDOVICK, born 1787, was at Ratisbon Seminary in 1800. [SIG#295][RSC#I.254]

REID, WILLIAM, was educated at the Scots College in Rome in 1661, then a Benedictine in Ratisbon. [SF#275]

REID, WILLIAM, a suspected priest who had returned to Scotland from Ratisbon or Windsburg, was imprisoned in Aberdeen Tolbooth in 1690. [RPCS.XVI.469]

REIDTLER, HANS, a merchant in Hamburg, 1674. [NRS.AC7.5]

REITH, BENEDICT, from Aberdeen, admitted to the Monastery of Ratisbon on 15 May 1650. died in the Monastery of Herbipolis in 1684. [SIG#292]

RENNY, JAMES, a merchant in Hamburg, admitted as a burgess of Montrose in 1767. [Montrose Burgess Roll]

RENTOUN, JOHN, a Major General of the Swedish Army in Germany during the 1630s. [SIG#283]

REYNICK, WALTER, master of the St Laurence of Lubeck captured by Sir William Alexander before 1631. [RPCS.IV.375]

RHODE, JOHANNES RUDOLPHUS JAPHETS, from Germany, for 30 years a surgeon of the British Army, graduated MD at King's College, Aberdeen, on 14 June 1793. [KCA#139]

RIDDELL, ARCHIBALD, assistant commissary general in British Service, married Leopoldine, daughter of the late M. de Lindenheime, in Vienna on 24 November 1836. [DPCA#1779]

RIEDAL, J. GUSTAV, born in Strasland, Prussia, during 1794, a shipmaster, died at sea, buried in Dundee on 18 April 1836. [Dundee Burial Register]

RITCHIE, ALEXANDER, in Prussia, granted a birth brief in 1641 by Aberdeen burgh council. [APB]

RITZING, ..., minister of Emden, 1683. [NRS.NRAS.3564, MS box 1/9/1-17]

ROBERTSON, EDWARD, son of John Robertson and his wife Margaret Crag at the Mill of Corsinday, settled in Riesenberg, Prussia, by 1585. [APB]

ROBERTSON, Captain DAVID, in Hamburg circa 1630. [NA.SP75.13, FF233-235]

ROBERTSON, GEORGE, eldest son of the late John Robertson, secretary to King George I as Elector of Hanover, descended from the Robertons of Roberton and Earnock in Lanarkshire, pedigree 20 June 1730. [NRS.Lyon Office, GI.14]

ROBERTSON, JAMES, from Edinburgh, a student at the University of Heidelberg, matriculated on 17 April 1589. [SIG#314][SHR.V.67]

ROBERTSON, JAMES, from Edinburgh, a student at the University of Heidelberg, 1589. [RCPE]

ROBERTSON, JAMES, born 20 October 1758, was at Ratisbon Seminary in 1772, ordained as a priest on 27 October 1782, died 3 May 1820. [SIG#295] [RSC#I.253]; Reverend James Robertson, Strahfeld, Ratisbon, Bavaria, probate 16 December 1820. [NA.Prob.11/1637]

ROBERTSON, JOHN, a merchant in Leith, married Margaret Elizabeth Moller, daughter of J. J. Moller in Hamburg, in North Leith on 17 October 1817. [BEM.II.244]

ROBERTSON, WILLIAM, born 5 December 1824, was at the Ratisbon Seminary in 1838, the last Scottish monk at Ratisbon, died in Fochabers, Morayshire, on 19 November 1900. [SIG#295][RSC#I.256]

ROBERTSON, ..., son of Robert Robertson the younger of Auchleeks, was born in Heidelberg on 17 October 1854. [W.XV.1593]

ROBERTSON and Company, merchants in Hamburg, 1805.

[NRS.B59.37.4.3/4]

ROCHEID, CHARLES, of Inverleith, died in Dresden on 19 January 1864, inventory, 1864, Commissariat of Edinburgh. [NRS]

ROCHEID, JAMES, of Inverleith, married Sarah Catherine Patterson, only daughter of the late William Patterson from London, in Frankfort on 31 January 1837. [DPCA#1803]

ROLLAND, JOSEPH, was admitted to the Monastery of Ratisbon in 1734. [SIG#294]

ROLLAND, WILLIAM, was at Ratisbon Seminary in 1772. [SIG#295][RSC#I.253]

ROSE, GEORGE K., in Berlin, 1793. [NRS.NRAS#3955/60/1/356]

ROSE, JAMES, a merchant traveller in Germany, 1630. [NRS.GD34/453]

ROSS, AMBROSE, from Ross, was admitted to the Monastery of Ratisbon on 25 February 1708, died 1714. [SIG#293]

ROSS, HERCULES, in Wellingsbuttel, Hamburg, died on 11 September 1845, inventory, 1846, Commissariat of Edinburgh. [NRS]

ROSS, JOHN, a merchant in Hamburg, 1795. [NRS.GD51.1.496]

ROWAN, JAMES, [Jakob Rowan], born in Greifswald, a pharmacist in Anklam by 1672, a councillor there in 1693, died there in 1717. [HKA]

ROWAN, WILLIAM, a merchant and councillor in Anklam, near Greifswald, died there in 1616. [HKA]

ROWAN, WILLIAM, [Wilhelm Rowan], born in Anklam during 1582, a merchant and 'civis primarius' in Anklam, near

Greifswald, died in Greifswald after 1664. [HKA]

ROY, CHARLES, was at Ratisbon Seminary in 1772.
[SIG#295][RSC#I.253]

RUSSEL, ALEXANDER, from Aberdeen, a student at the
University of Greifswald, 1519. [SIG#313]

RUSSEL, JAMES, born 3 August 1815, was at the Ratisbon
Seminary in 1830, died in Glasgow during 1837.
[SIG#295][RSC#I.255]

RUTHERFORD, ANDREW, a General of the Swedish Army in
Germany, 1630s. [SIG#282]

RUTHERFORD, JOHN CHATTO, youngest son of William
Oliver Rutherford of Edgerston, Roxburghshire, died in
Crewzuach, Rhenish Prussia, on 4 July 1857.
[W.XVIII.1889]

RUTHVEN, Colonel FRANCIS, a military officer in Hamburg,
1639. [SSNE#3404]

RUTHVEN, Sir J., a Colonel of the Swedish Army in Germany
during the 1630s. [SIG#283]

RUTHVEN, Colonel PATRICK, (1573-1651), Governor of
Ulm, 1632-1633. [STW#288][MGIF.Map 3][SIG#282]

SADDLER, DAVID, died in Worms, Germany, before December
1744, husband of Christian Cornwall. [SLIR#665]

SALT, PETER, born 1735 in Mollon, Hanover, a sugar refiner in
Hamburg, moved to England in 1757, by 1798 residing in
Canongate, Edinburgh. [ECA.SL115.2.1/105]

SALOMON, JULIUS, merchant in Dundee, married Adele,
eldest daughter of Ludolph Schwabe, at 78 Grindel,
Hamburg, by Reverend Dr Sachs on 21 July 1869 in
Hamburg. [PJD.604]

SALVESEN, FREDERIKKE MARIE, second daughter of J. T. Salvesen of Polmont House, died at Freizenbad, Bohemia, on 4 September 1873. [GH#10513]

SANTFOLLEN, ANTONIO, born 1775 in Innsbruck, Tirol, a mason, landed at Leith on 23 October 1817, resident there by October 1817. [ECA.SL115.2.2/80]

SCARTH, FANNY, eldest daughter of Thomas Scarth, married Captain William Hamilton Ramsay of the 1st Royal Lanark Militia, at the British Embassy in Dresden on 27 August 1857. [W.XVIII.1902]

SCHACK, EDWARD, Baron de, born in Vienna, educated in Prague and Vienna, graduated MD from St Andrews University in 1822, settled in the West Indies, died at La Guayra on 1 September 1824. [SAUR]

SCHAFF, PHILIP, born 1 January 1819, son of Philip Schaff a carpenter in Chur, Switzerland, educated at Tubingen, Halle, and Berlin, graduated DD from St Andrews in 1887, died in New York 1893. [SAUR]

SCHAFFER, JOSEPH, from Bohemia, a medical graduate of Edinburgh University, 1807. [EMG#40]

SCHEUCH, FREDERICK, born 1812 in Offenbach, a lithographer in Edinburgh by 1851. [Census]

SCHETKY, JOHN ALEXANDER, a surgeon, former apprentice to Thomas Wood a surgeon burgess, was admitted as a burgess of Edinburgh on 13 June 1818. [EBR]

SCHETKY, JOHN GEORGE CHRISTOPHER, son of Frederic Schetky and his wife ... McPherson or Voghel, from Hesse-Darmstadt, a musician, settled in Edinburgh during 1772, married Maria Theresa Reinagle, daughter of Joseph Reinagle the state trumpeter, parents of Charles (a surgeon who died in India), George (who emigrated to

America), Caroline (who settled in Boston), John Christian, and John Alexander. [SGen.XXVI.94]

SCHLESELMAN, JAMES, born 1867 in Dundee, son of George Schleselman and Mary Henderson, student 1885-1889. [SAUR]

SCHLESELMAN, PETER, a sugar refiner in Dundee, dead by 1834. [NRS.CE70.11.4.50]

SCHLUTER, FREDRICK, of Hamburg, was admitted as an honorary burgess and guilds-brother of Glasgow on 15 November 1779. [Glasgow Burgess Roll]

SCHMIDT, MARCUS MAXIMILIAN, born in Austria, graduated MD from Glasgow University in 1861, [RGG]

SCHMIDT, or MAHLSTEDT, MARION, wife of Luder Mahlstedt, a farmer in Hagen, Hanover, was serviced as heir to her mother Jane Irving or Schmidt, wife of Arp Schmidt, in Stellerbruch near Bremen, who died on 29 October 1831, on 28 December 1849. [NRS.SH]

SCHMITZ, CAROL THEODORE, from England, a medical graduate of Edinburgh University, 1858. [EMG#165]

SCHMITZ, LEONARD, LL.D., born 1807 in Prussia, Rector of Edinburgh High School by 1851. [Census]

SCHNEIDER, JOHN, born 1784, died in Neuchatel, Switzerland, on 5 May 1859, father of M. C. H. Schnieder of the High School of Edinburgh. [S#1214]

SCHOMBERG, MENHARDUS, Count, was admitted as a burgess and guilds-brother of Ayr on 4 December 1689. [ABR]

SCHONEIR, MARTIN, married Christian Gibson in Edinburgh in 1601. [Edinburgh Marriage Register]

SCHONHER, FERDINAND, born during 1774 in Bremen, a tailor in Lisbon, then in London, and by 1798 in Edinburgh. [ECA.SL115.2.1/156]

SCHRINE, JOHN, from Aberdeen, a student at the University of Rostock in 1592. [SIG#313]

SCHUBERT, JOTT LOB FREDERICK, married Margaret Forbes in Musselburgh on 22 December 1769. [Musselburgh Marriage Register]

SCHULER, DANIEL, a musician from Essweiler, Kusel, died in Dundee during 1863. [NRS.NRAS.3250/53]

SCHULTIN, HEINRICH, master of the St Marie of Lubeck, 1628. [NRS.AC7.1.149]

SCHULTZE, ALEXANDER, from Scotland, a medical graduate of Edinburgh University, 1850, [EMG#148]; MD, son of Alexander Schultze a merchant in Leith, died in Dunkeld, Mount Sturgeon, Victoria, on 19 November 1858. [W.XX.2059]

SCHULTZE, FREDERICK, born 1764 in Brandenburg, a staymaker, moved to London in 1788, a resident of 8 Leith Street, Edinburgh, by 1798. [ECA.SL115.2.1/70]; married Helen Ramsay in Edinburgh on 14 July 1791. [Edinburgh Marriage Register]

SCHULTZE, FREDERICK, Ramsay Place, Newhaven, Edinburgh, died on 18 February 1844. [NRS. Inventories of Personal Estates, Edinburgh, 1846]

SCHULTZE, FREDERICK, eldest son of Alexander Schultze, a merchant, died at 1 Vanburgh Place, Leith, on 27 January 1854. [W.XV.1513]

SCHULTZE, HEINRICH, master of the Fortune of Hamburg, 1629. [NRS.AC7.1.238]

SCHULTZE, JOHANN FRIEDRICH, born 1762 in Berlin, a staymaker in Leith by 1798. [ECA.SL115.2.1/44]

SCHULTZ, LAURENCE, master of the Fortune of Hamburg, February 1629. [NRS.AC7.1]

SCHUSTER, CHRISTIAN FRIEDERICH ALBERT, married Sarah Archer in Edinburgh in 1853. [Edinburgh Marriage Register]

SCHWABE, SALIS, son of E. H. Schwabe a merchant in Oldenburg, and a merchant of the house of M. W. Schwabe and Company, merchants, 74 Buchanan Street, Glasgow, was admitted a burgess and guildsbrother of Glasgow, by purchase, on 30 March 1832. [Glasgow Burgess Roll]

SCHWARTZ, AUGUST FERDINAND CARL, an inventory, 1871. [NRS.SC70.151.588]

SCHWEITZER, SERAVIN, married Marc Ferenbach in Edinburgh on 6 June 1839. [St Cuthbert's Marriage Register]

SCOTT, ALEXANDER, sergeant in the Prince of Hesse's Regiment, a deed, 1693. [NRS.RD4.72.1155]

SCOTT, ALEXANDER, was at the Ratisbon Seminary in 1830, died in Rome on 16 April 1839. [SIG#295][RSC#I.255]

SCOTT, ALEXANDER, in Fiume, Austria, died on 18 November 1860, inventory, 1865, Commissariat of Edinburgh. [NRS]

SCOTT, CHARLES H., in Frankfort on Maine, 1839. [NRS.RD5.1095.169]

SCOTT, HUGH, of Harden, and Harriet Bruhl, daughter of Hans Moritz, Count de Bruhl, a marriage contract, 1795. [NRS.GD157.1584]

SCOTT, HUGH FRANCIS, son of Hugh Scott, in Dresden during 1823. [NRS.GD157/2359]

SCOTT, JAMES, a student at the Scots College in Douai around 1620, to Wurzburg in 1623. [SF#274]

SCOTT, LEONARD, married Mary Lee in the English Church of Hamburg on 21 July 1646.[TKH]; a merchant in Hamburg, 1652. [NRS.GD57.1.336/10]

SCOTT, LEONARD, a merchant in Hamburg, 1652. [NRS.GD57.336.10]

SCOTT, VENTIS, Captain of Bligh's Foot, Neuwied, Electorate of Treves, probate 17 May 1745. [NA.Prob.11/740]

SCOTT, ..., daughter of Charles Stewart Scott, was born in Darmstadt, Germany, on 26 February 1879. [S#11,118]

SEATON, ALEXANDER, Governor of Stralsund, 1628. [MGIF. Map 3]

SEATON, GREGORY, born 1658, died before ordination in Ratisbon on 13 February 1685. [SF#280]

SEILLAR, JOHN, a paper maker at Dalry, 1595. [NRS.RD1.50.342]

SEITZ, CARL DIETRICH JULIUS, in Funchal, Madeira, an inventory, 1875. [NRS.SC70.174.942]

SELBY, HANS or JOHN, a small trader in Wismar 1597 to 1602. [SIG#51]

SELIGER, ..., daughter of Carl Gustav Seliger, was born in Potsdam on 12 October 1860. [S#1663]

SERVICE, GEORGE, from Saltcoats, Ayrshire, a prisoner in Emden 1796. [NRS.NRAS.3955.60.3/78]

SETON, DAVID, from the Diocese of Aberdeen, matriculated at the University of Koln in 1422. [SNQ.X.3/77]

SETON, DAVID, educated at the Braunsberg Seminary around 1609. [SIG#299]

SETON, JAMES, educated at the Braunsberg Seminary around 1609. [SIG#299]

SETON, Sir JOHN, of Carchunoth, a soldier in Bohemia, 1619-1620. [STW#111]; Governor of Trebon, 1620-1622. [MGIF.Map 3]

SHARP, PETER, born 29 December 1769 in Mortlach, was at Ratisbon Seminary in 1784. [SIG#295][RSC#I.254]

SHAW, JAMES, born in Portsoy, Banffshire, on 10 October 1837, was at the Ratisbon Seminary in 1852, returned to Scotland. [SIG#296][RSC#I.258]

SHAW, JOHN, born in Gollachie, near Buckie, Banffshire, on 15 August 1833, was at the Ratisbon Seminary in 1845, ordained as a priest and returned to Scotland in 1862. [SIG#296] [RSC#I.258]

SHAW, JOHN, born in Gollachie near Portsoy, Banffshire, on 15 August 1833, was at the Ratisbon Seminary in 1852. [SIG#296] [RSC#I.257]

SHEARER, MICHAEL, born 1740 in Schwartzwald, landed in Kirkcaldy, Fife, in 1759, a wooden clockmaker in Lawnmarket, Edinburgh, around 1790. [ECA.SL115.2.1/41]

SHEARER, PATRICK, son of William Shearer and his wife Janet Brown in Auchenleck, Kinnoir, a resident of Elbing, Prussia, 1599. [APB]

SHIELLS, ELIZA J., 13 Albrechts Casse, Dresden, 7 July 1868. [NRS.B22.4.94.254]

SHORTREDE, ANDREW, proprietor of the *China Mail*, died in Bad Bruckenaw, Bavaria, 31 August 1858, Comm. Edinburgh. [NRS]

SIBBALD, DAVID, son of John Sibbald of Keir and his wife Janet Strachan, a Lieutenant Colonel in Swedish service, was killed in Germany in September 1641. [APB]

SIBBALD, JOHN, in Prussia, son of John Sibbald of Keir and his wife Janet Strachan, a soldier in Swedish service who fought in Germany, was issued with a birth brief by Aberdeen burgh council on 2 May 1642. [APB]

SIBSON, JOHN, sometime of Downhill Academy, Durham, died in Hamburg, 1 March 1850, inventory, 1851, Comm. Edinburgh. [NRS]

SIMONS, ISAAC, a merchant in Hamburg, a deed of factory to Robert Sandilands a merchant in Edinburgh, 1669. [NRS.RD4.9.1851]

SIMPSON, ADAM, a student at the Scots College in Douai around 1588, and by 1598 was a monk at Ratisbon. [SF#274]

SIMPSON, ANTHONY, a merchant in Hamburg, 1743-1753. [NRS.AC8.661; GD144/209]

SIMSON, ANDREW, from the Diocese of Aberdeen, matriculated at the University of Koln in 1494. [SNQ.X.3/78]

SIMSON, HANS, a merchant in Greifswald, Pomerania, around 1540. [SGen.XXVII.4]

SIMSON, MARY ANN, eldest daughter of the late John Brook Simson, married Alexander J. D. Dorsey, in Berlin on 13 July 1835. [GA#XXXV.5101]

SIMSON, THOMAS, son of James Simson, a burgess of

Aberdeen, and his wife Christian Cults, died in
Williamsburg, Neumark, before August 1592. [APB]

SINCLAIR, ANDREW, ("ANDREAS SINCKLER"), member of
the Shetland Company in Hamburg, around 1610.
[SAH/VDHS]

SINCLAIR, FR., a Colonel of the Swedish Army in Germany
during the 1630s. [SIG#283]

SINCLAIR, JOHN, son of the Earl of Caithness, a Colonel of the
Swedish Army in Germany during the 1630s, died at
Neumark in the Palatinate. [SIG#283]

SINCLAIR, JOHN, in Berlin, 1709. [NRS.GD24.3.245]

SINCLAIR, ("STINCKLER"), **LAURENCE,** member of the
Shetland Company in Hamburg, around 1593.
[SAH/VDHS]

SINCLAIR, THOMAS, ("THOMAS SENCKLER"), member of
the Shetland Company in Hamburg, around 1626.
[SAH/VDHS]

SINCLAIR, ..., son of Lady Sinclair of Murkle, was born in
Mannheim on 13 August 1835. [DPCA#1728]

SINSERF, THOMAS or JOHN, a student at the University of
Heidelberg, 1609. [RCPE]

SKENE, ALFRED, of Pawlowitz-Prerau in Austria, descended
from Peter Skene from Midmar, Aberdeenshire, who settled in
Venloo, Holland, certificate, 20 July 1888. [NRS.Lyon
Office.G.III.37]

SKENE, JOHN, in Hamburg, 14 September 1590, wrote to King
Christian IV of Denmark. [DAC]

SKENE, JOHN, a student at the University of Helmstadt in 1593.
[SIG#313]

SKINNER, Captain DAVID, died in Weimar, Saxony, on 13 Aug.1828, inventory, 1829, C

SKIRVING, HELEN, wife of the Reverend R. H. Herschell in London, died in Bonn, inventory, 31 December 1853, with the Commissariat of Edinburgh. [NRS]

SMITH, GEORGE, late merchant in Hamburg, died in December 1834, inventory, 1839, Comm. Edinburgh. [NRS]

SMITH, JAMES, from Glasgow, in Hamburg, a letter, 1802. [NRS.NRAS.1684.6.1]

SMITH, JAMES, graduated BA in 1846 and MA in 1847 from Glasgow University, minister of the English Reformed Church in Hamburg. [RGG]

SMITH, JOHN, a mariner born in Danzig, Prussia, and his wife Isabella Henderson, were parents of children born in Dundee – Ann in 1814, William in 1815, and John in 1817. [Dundee Episcopal baptismal register]

SMITH, JOHN GUTHRIE, from Glasgow, fourth son of William Smith of Carbeth-Guthrie, married Anne Penelope Campbell Dennistoun, daughter of James Robert Dennistoun, at the British Embassy, Stuttgart, on 26 January 1861. [W.XXII.2272]

SMYTH, GILBERT, son of William Smyth and his wife Janet Davidson in Ardconan, Bathelny, Aberdeenshire, settled in Prussia by 1603. [APB]

SOUTAR, WILLIAM, a traveller in Germany and Danzig, son of David Soutar and his wife Elizabeth Lindsay, Dundee birth brief dated 11 March 1609. [Dundee Burgh Archives]

SPALDING, ANDREW, settled in Plau near Mecklenburg about 1600, and became a member of the Senate, his son became a burgomaster, and his grandson Thomas moved to Gustrow [SIG#50/315]

SPALDING, EDWARD AUGUSTUS, auf Gloedenhof im Kriese Griefswald, certificate. [NRS.Lyon Office #G.III.57]

SPENCE, ANDREW, a citizen of Bremen, was admitted thus on 17 November 1636. [StAB Burgerbuch der Alstadt, 1622-1642]

SPENCE, GILBERT, a merchant in Bremen, 1699. [NRS.RD3.91.651]

SPENCE, Sir JAMES, General of the Swedish Army in Germany, 1630s. [SIG#282]

SPENS, GILBERT, a merchant in Bremen, deeds, 1676, 1679. [NRS.GD29/1906; RD2.47.745; RD2.48.648]

SPIERS, MARGARET BRUCE, daughter of the late Archibald Spiers of Elderslie, died in Wiesbaden on 12 November 1858. [W.XIX.2034]

SPINDLER, GEORGE, born 1760 in Melhausen, Saxony, arrived in London during 1783, butler to Drummond of Megginch, Perthshire, by 1798. [ECA.SL115.2.1/79]

SPRECKELSEN, FRANS FERDINAND, in Hamburg, an inventory, 1874. [NRS.SC70.166.649]

SPROT, MARK GEORGE, late Captain of the 93rd Highlanders, second son of Mark Sprot of Riddell, Roxburghshire, died in Villeneuve, Lake Geneva, on 16 September 1859. [W.XX.2125]

STALKER, THOMAS, settled in Danzig before 1594. [RPCS.V.214]

STEILL, WILLIAM, a merchant in Hamburg, 1591. [EBR; 20 May 1591]

STEINHAUR, JOHN IGNATIUS, from England, a medical graduate of Edinburgh University, 1799. [EMG#30]

STEPHEN, JAMES, a merchant in Hamburg, 1714.
[NRS.AC8.169]

STEPHEN, JAMES, a merchant in Hamburg, 1744,
[NRS.AC8.638]; letters, 1743-1754, [NRS.NRAS#2594];
was admitted as a burgess of Montrose in 1753. [Montrose
Burgess Roll]

STEPHEN, ..., in Hamburg, 1771-1772. [NRS.NRAS#1368,
bundle 74]

STEPHEN, Sir JAMES, Professor of Modern History at the
University of Cambridge, died in Koblentz on 14 September
1859. [W.XX.2124]

STEPHEN, JOHN, a merchant in Hamburg, 1751.
[NRS.RD4.177/2.577]

STEVEN, ALEXANDER, son of William Steven and his wife
Elspet Moir in Drumnahoy, Cluny, a traveller in Prussia,
1599. [APB]

STEVENSON, ["STEFFENSEN"], ALEXANDER, from St
Andrews, Scotland, married Barbara Cornelis, in Hamburg
during 1608. [TKH]

STEVENSON, GABRIEL, a merchant in Hamburg, was serviced
as heir to his mother Mary Fleming or Stevenson who died
on 27 April 1842, on 22 May 1850. [NRS.SH]

STEWART, ALEXANDER, co-founder of the Prussian East
India Company of Emden, 1740s.

STEWART, FRANCIS, third child of Francis Stewart, (1674-
1739), and Jean Elphinstone, Lieutenant Colonel of
Honeywood's Dragoons, who died in Germany on 28
August 1760. [SP.VI.324]

STEWART, GEORGE, married Magdalen Williames in the
English Church of Hamburg on 20 April 1624. [TKH]

STEWART, HENRY, fifth child of Francis Stewart, (1674-1739), and Jean Elphinstone, a major in the Army who died in Germany. [SP.VI.325]

STEWART, JANE, in Hamburg, 1620

STEWART, JOHN, son of Archibald Stewart, a citizen of Old Aberdeen, and his wife Isobel Chalmer, a traveller in Germany, 1595. [APB]

STEWART, JOHN, son of John Stewart of Boggs, a Colonel in Imperial German Service, 1793. [NRS.S/H]

STEWART, WILLIAM, brother of the Earl of Traquair, a Colonel of the Swedish Army in Germany during the 1630s. [SIG#283]

STEWART, ..., a Captain of the Swedish Army in Germany during the 1630s. [SIG#283]

STIRLER, ..., a Lieutenant of Brigadier Slirler's Regiment of Swiss, was admitted as a burgess and guildsbrother of Glasgow on 26 June 1719. [GBR]

STIRLING, JANE, daughter of Reverend James Stirling in Aberdeen, died at Bel Alp, Switzerland, on 15 July 1884. [S#31147]

STIRLING, MARY ANN, wife of Sir Samuel Stirling of Glorat, died in Friedrichshaffen, Lake Constance, on 8 October 1856. [W.XVII.1811]

STITCHILL, PATRICK, was educated at the Braunsberg Seminary around 1607, became a Jesuit. [SIG#299]

STOLTEFELT, PETER, master of the <u>Pelican of Wismar</u>, 1677. [NRS.AC7.4]

STRACHAN, MAURICE, matriculated at Wurzburg on 6 November 1694, studied metaphysics. [SF#272]

STRACHAN, MARY ANNE, wife of J. C. Tozer of Cliffden, died in Schwalbach, Germany, on 22 September 1857. [W.XVIII.1914]

STRACHAN, ROBERT, from Montrose, Angus, was educated at the Scots College in Rome from 1634 to 1638, then a Benedictine in Wurzburg. [SF#275, 280]

STRATFORD, FRANCIS, a merchant in Hamburg, 1697. [NRS.RD3.87.623]

STREIBER, AUGUSTUS, from Eisenae, Saxony, was admitted as a burgess of Montrose, Angus, in 1790, also as a burgess of Arbroath, Angus, in 1790. [MBR][ArBR]

STUART, ALEXANDER, at the Ratisbon Seminary in 1718. [SIG#294][RSC#I.250]

STUART, ANTONY, son of the laird of Lismurden, was admitted to the Monastery of Ratisbon on 26 September 1726. [SIG#293]

STUART, BERNARD, son of the laird of Boggs, was admitted to the Monastery of Ratisbon on 26 September 1726. [SIG#293]

STUART, CHARLES, born 27 August 1709, matriculated at the Ratisbon Seminary in 1719. [SIG#294][RSC#I.251]

STUART, CHARLES, born 1817, second son of Major General P. Stuart, was drowned at Interlaken, Switzerland, on 30 July 1835. [DPCA#1726]

STUART, CHRISTIAN ERSKINE, third daughter of J. A. Stuart, and grand-daughter of the late Charles Stuart of Dunairn, MD, married Wilhelm Theodor Biberauer, only son of Reverend Michael Biberauer, at the Protestant Church in Graz on 14 February 1857. [W.XVIII.1845]

STUART, JAMES, at the Ratisbon Seminary in 1718.

[SIG#294][RSC#I.250]

STUART, JAMES, born 1734, matriculated at the Ratisbon
Seminary in 1747. [SIG#294][RSC#I.252]

STUART, JOHN, matriculated at Wurzburg on 5 March 1598.
[SF#272]

STUART, JOHN, born near Glasgow, professed at Ratisbon
before 1595, died in May 1614. [ASF#279]

STUART, JOHN, at the Ratisbon Seminary in 1713.
[SIG#294][RSC#I.250]

STUART, JOHN, born 1731, at the Ratisbon Seminary in 1747.
[SIG#294][RSC#I.252]

STUART, JOHN, born on 16 July 1822, was at the Ratisbon
Seminary in 1838, later a missionary in Scotland, died in
Glasgow on 12 January 1875. [SIG#295][RSC#I.256]

STUART, JOHN ALEXANDER, born 1787, late of Carnock,
Fife, died in Dresden on 3 November 1869. [PJ]

STUART, MAURICE, of Ainia, Diocese of Aberdeen, was
admitted to the Monastery of Ratisbon on 1 August 1692, a
Professor in Prague by 1697, died 1720. [SIG#293]

STUART, PATRICK, at the Ratisbon Seminary in 1719.
[SIG#294][RSC#I.251]

STUART, WILLIAM, in Hamburg, 14 September 1590, wrote to
King Christian IV of Denmark. [DAC]

STUART, WILLIAM, born 1 December 1826, was at the
Ratisbon Seminary in 1838, returned to Scotland in 1845.
[SIG#295][RSC#I.256]

SUEMAN, HERMAN, a merchant in Bremen, 1601. [SD2.327]

SUSS, or LOWE, Mrs HELEN M., in Treves, Prussia, an inventory, 1878. [NRS.SC70.189.306]

SWANSON, ANDREW, a merchant, 1625. [SSNE#6288]

SWART, MATTIAS, master of the White Unicorn of Hamburg, 1630. [NRS.AC7.1.278]

SYDSERF, PATRICK, sergeant major of Colonel Sir James Ramsay in Germany, dead by 28 May 1634. [EBR; 28.5.1634]

SYDSERF, THOMAS, matriculated at the University of Heidelberg on 10 July 1609. [SHR.V.67]

TAILFEIR, JAMES, a merchant, was sent to Hamburg by Edinburgh Town Council in 1649. [EBR: 28 March 1649]

TALLIFER, JAMES, in Hamburg, 1653. [NRS.GD18.2524]

TAYLOR, HENRY, married Elizabeth Dogett, in Hamburg, 1634. [TKH]

THIERGAERTNER, or DRUMMOND, Mrs MARIA WALKER, former wife of F.A.Thiergaertner in Baden, died 24 January 1858, Comm. Edinburgh. [NRS]

THOMSON, JAMES, born in Cumnock, Ayrshire, during 1844, graduated MA from Glasgow University in 1874, died in Badenweiler, Germany, on 3 August 1876. [RGG]

THOMSON, JOHN, educated at the Braunsberg Seminary around 1580, died there in 1588. [SIG#299]

THOMSON, ["THOMESSEN"], JOHN, from Carron, Stirlingshire, married Agatha Cornelis from Hamburg, there in 1636. [TKH]

THOMSON, ["TOMMASON"], JOHN, a Scots captain in the service of Hamburg, 1660. [JTA.102]

THOMSON, THOMAS, Governor of Hagelburg, 1638.
[MGIF.Map 3]

TIMINS, MIERS, a seal-maker from Breslau, Prussia, who
settled in Edinburgh around 1794. [ECA.Aliens Register]

TOD, RICHARD, a student at the Scots College in Douai who
went to Wurzburg in 1623; matriculated there on 12 June
1625, studied physics, dead by 1635. [SF#272-274-279]

TOMLOE, JOHN, a merchant in Hamburg, 1698.
[NRS.RD2.81/1.647]; his testament was confirmed in 1730
with the Commissariat of Edinburgh. [NRS]

TRAILL, ANNE, probably from Orkney, in Hamburg around
1851. [NRS.GD263/104]

TRAILL, ANNE FOTHERINGHAM, in Baden near Vienna,
heir to her uncle William Henry Fotheringham, sheriff clerk
of Orkney, who died on 13 October 1868, 12 January 1870.
[NRS.S/H]

TRAILL, THOMAS, and his wife Anne Fotheringham, probably
from Orkney, in Mannheim, 1825. [NRS.GD263/88/1-2-3]

TROTTER, SARAH JANE, daughter of William Trotter of
Ballindean, married Charles, Baron de Lancken,
chamberlain to the Elector of Hesse, in Franckfort-on-
Maine on 15 May 1844. [W.V.466]

TSHARNER, ..., a Lieutenant of Brigadier Slirler's Regiment
of Swiss, was admitted as a burgess and guildsbrother of
Glasgow on 26 June 1719. [GBR]

TULLOCH, ALEXANDER, a Captain of the Swedish Army in
Germany during the 1630s. [SIG#283]

TURNER, JAMES, a student at Frankfurt-on-the-Oder in 1582.
[SIG#313]

TURNER, WILLIAM, son of John Turner and his wife Margaret Collie in Glesfennie, Drumoak, Kincardineshire, a traveller in Prussia, 1591. [APB]

TWEEDALE, SUSAN ROSE, daughter of Captain James Tweedale late of the East India Company's Service, married the Reverend Charles Lushington, son of Sir Henry Lushington, in Berne on 28 July 1835. [DPCA#1728]

UHDE, CHARLES, of Handschuheim, married Olympia Campbell, second daughter of Sir Alexander Cockburn Campbell, and grand-daughter of Major General Sir John Malcolm, in Wiesbaden on 4 November 1857. [W.XVIII.1924]

UHDE, CHARLES ADOLPHUS, of Handschuheim, Heidelberg, died 17 November 1856, inventory 1857, Commissariat of Edinburgh, [NRS]

URQUHART, ANDREW, a monk at the Monastery of St James, Wurzburg before 1630. [SF#279]

URQUHART, F. E. POLLARD, in Berlin and Hamburg, 1821. [NRS.NRAS.2570, bundle 69]

VAN DER BERGE, ANTHONY, a merchant in Hamburg, 1675. [NRS.RD3.40.33]

VAN DER HASON, BARTRAM, a merchant in Hamburg, 1709. [NRS.AC9.337]

VAN DER MEDEN, DANIEL, partner of the Nightingale of Bremen, 1673. [NRS.RD3.33.721]

VAN DER SYDE, DAVID, master of the St Isobel of Hamburg, December 1627. [NRS.AC7.1]

VAN DOORNE, CRYNE, master of the St Peter of Stadt, 1677. [NRS.AC7.4]

VAN HUYSEN, BERTRAM, a merchant in Hamburg, 1707.
[NRS.AC10.56]

VAN PARTEN, PHILIP, a merchant in Hamburg, 1674.
[NRS.AC7.4]

VAN SOME, THEODORE, and his son Henry, merchants in
Hamburg, 1674. [NRS.AC7.5]

VAN WEED, CORNELIUS, a merchant in Hamburg, was
admitted as a burgess and guilds-brother of Aberdeen on 16
March 1633 and of Edinburgh in 1679. [ABR/EBR]; deeds,
1684. [NRS.RD2.63.484; RD4.53.851]

VAN WYNGARDEN, JOHANNES, in Hamburg, 1749.
[NRS.AC9.1661]

VERNON, FRANCIS, in Lubeck, 1632, [NRS.GD406.1.102];
agent for the 3rd Marquis of Hamilton in Bremen, ca.1651.
[NRS.NRAS#2177/bundle 2829]

VICK, HEINRICH, master of the St Eric of Lubeck, 21 July
1628. [NRS.AC7.1.164]

VINAZER, CHRISTIAN, born during 1779 in the Tirol,
emigrated from Hamburg to Leith, settled in the Canongate,
Edinburgh, by 1798. [ECA.SL115.2.1/132]

VIPPERMAN, JOHN, steersman of the King David of Hamburg,
17 January 1683. [NRS.RD3.55.183]

VITALES, Mrs B., born 1823 in Germany, a servant in
Edinburgh by 1851. [Census]

VOELTZEKE, JOHANN JACOB, born during 1763 in Berlin, a
surgeon in Prussian service, arrived at Harwich on 19 May
1803, residing at 5 Rose Street, Edinburgh, by December
1803. [ECA.SL115.2.2/29]

VON BRUSBERG, HERMINA, born in Koln, wife of Peter

Leenders, also born in Koln, a merchant in Copenhagen, and their daughters Christina and Emilia, in Leith in September 1672. [NRS.AC7.3.198]

VON BUXHATAUSS, CONRADT, in Berlin, a letter to the Marquis of Hamilton, 1636. [NRS.GD406.1.9652]

VON GUMPPENBERG, JANE B., widow (?) of Baron Pottries, a Lieutenant of the Bavarian Army, deeds, 1886. [NRS.RD5.2063.234.67; 2063.261.67]

VON JOXHEIM, JOBST WILLIAM, possibly from Hamburg, was admitted as a burgess of Glasgow on 3 June 1735. [GBR]

VON KROSIGK, GERHARD ADOLPH FRIEDRICH, lord of Hoken, Erxleben, Prussia, died 3 March 1856, inventory, 1857, Comm. Edinburgh. [NRS]

VON NORMANN, Baron WILHELMTHEODOR, of New Strelitz, Mecklenburg-Strelitz, Secretary to the Prussian Delegation in Hamburg, and Wilmina Marianne Douglas MacLean Clephane of Carslogie and Torluisk, Argyll, antenuptial marriage contract, 1831. [NRS.GD2.426]

VON PIERSON, CAROLINE MATHILDE OLGA, daughter of Woldemar von Pierson, genealogy, 10 October 1900. [NRS. Lyon Office. GIII/54]

VON PIERSON, SOPHIE ANNA, daughter of Woldemar von Pierson, genealogy, 10 October 1900. [NRS. Lyon Office. GIII/54]

VON WYNGARDEN, HENRY, a distiller in Edinburgh, a sasine, 14 January 1752. [NRS.RS27.139.218]

WAGNER, PHILIP, born during 1770 in Fieschbach, Germany, a gentleman's servant in Edinburgh by 1798. [ECA.SL115.2.1/61]

WAHLERS, CLAUS HINDRICH, born during 1786 in Hamburg, landed in Leith on 27 May 1816, a servant with Mr Cowan, papermaker in the Canongate, Edinburgh, by 6 June 1816. [ECA.SL115.2.2/77]

WALDICK, FREDERICK D., born in Berlin 1783, then in Paris, arrived in Portsmouth, a painter resident in Edinburgh by 1814. [ECA.SL115.2.2/73]

WALKER, ALEXANDER, son of James Walker, a burgess of Aberdeen, and his wife Constance Fenton, a burgess of Torun, Prussia, before 1591. [APB]

WALKER, THOMAS, son of John Walker and his wife Elizabeth Harvie in Disblair, a resident of "Sanctanberie", Germany, 1592. [APB]

WALKER, WILLIAM, son of John Walker and his wife Elizabeth Harvie in Disblair, a resident of "Sanctanberie", Germany, 1592. [APB]

WALKINGSHAW, JOHN, a Scottish gentleman in Germany, 1717. [HMC.Stuart pp.V.29]

WALLACE, CHARLES TENNANT, Captain of the 74th Highlanders, married Marie Karoline Hedwig, eldest daughter of Franz von Hunter-Amman a Major General of the Austrian Army, in Vienna on 18 February 1879. [S#11109]

WALLACE, Lady E., in Munich, 1799. [NRS.GD51.18.30]

WALLACE, GABRIEL, professed in the Monastery of St James, Wurzburg, before 1611, later possibly a lay-brother. [SF#279]

WALLACE, HUGH, from the Diocese of Glasgow, admitted to the Monastery of Ratisbon on 15 August 1606. [SIG#292]

WALLACE, EGLANTINE, Munich, probate 3 August 1803.

[NA.Prob.11/1398]

WALLACE, ..., son of Hamilton Gordon Wallace, was born in Hamburg on 8 November 1879. [Hawick Advertiser]

WATSON, HARRIET, in Frankfort-am-Maine, 22 April 1857. [NRS.B22.4.69.253]

WATSON, IRVINA, in Frankfort-am-Maine, 22 April 1857. [NRS.B22.4.69.253]

WATSON, or SCOTT, JESSIE, in Hamburg, was serviced as heir to her father the Reverend John Watson, Relief minister in Glasgow, on 20 November 1835. [NRS.SH]

WATSON, RICHARD, from Banff, matriculated at the University of Koln in 1480. [SNQ.X.3/48]

WATT, NICOL, [Nikel Watt], in Anklam, near Greifwald, 1608-1624. [HKA]

WATTENBACH, JOHAN GEORGE, from Hamburg, was admitted as a burgess of Montrose, Angus, in 1794. [MBR]

WAUCHOPE, SAMUEL B. C. S., in Switzerland, an inventory, 1877. [NRS.SC70.184.464]

WEBER, HENRY, born in St Petersburg during 1783, moved to Uhyst, Saxony, in 1788, arrived in Hull in 1797, a student of medicine at Edinburgh University in 1803, residing at Mrs Kerr's, Northside, St Patrick's Square. [ECA.SL115.2.2/22]

WEDDERBURN, GEORGE, from the Diocese of Aberdeen, was educated at the Scots College in Rome around 1623-1625, was admitted to the Monastery of Ratisbon on 8 December 1626. [SIG#292][SF#275]

WEIGEL, CHRISTIAN SHANFELD, born during 1776 in Greifswald, Pomerania, later resident of Stralsund,

Copenhagen and Gothenburg, a hairdresser, arrived at Harwich in June 1807, residing in West St Andrews Street, Edinburgh, by August 1807. [ECA.SL115.2.2/61]

WEIR, ROBERT, in Littmirritz, 1634. [NRS.GD406.1.9319]

WEIR, WILLIAM, a merchant in Hamburg, formerly in Edinburgh, 1772. [NRS.RS38.13.178]

WEMYSS, DAVID, second son of Major Wemyss of Wemyss Hall, Fife, married Marie de Waldkisch, daughter of Colonel de Waldkisch, from Schaffhausen, in Gothenburg on 9 June 1859. [W.XX.2115]

WESTPHALEN, HERMAN, in Hamburg, 1643. [NRS.GD84, Sec.2/195]

WESTSOILL, HANS, master of the JoNRS of Hamburg, 2 September 1628. [NRS.AC7.1.187]

WHISHAW, CHARLES, born on 13 January 1834, son of B. Whishaw in St Petersburg, educated at Glenalmond pre 1849, a merchant in Archangel, died in Germany on 29 June 1869. [SGS]

WHITTOCK, ALEXANDER MAXWELL, born in Edinburgh on 29 January 1834, died in Geneva on 23 November 1881. [Gullane MI, East Lothian]

WHITTON, ..., member of the Scottish Brotherhood at Greifswald, around 1600. [SIG#315]

WHYTE, HENRY ADAM, in Constadt, Germany, heir to his father Robert Whyte a cabinetmaker in Glasgow who died on 27 July 1861, 29 October 1868. [NRS.S/H]

WILLIAMS, JACOB, master of the Ewauld of Hamburg, 1628. [NRS.AC7.1.212]

WILLIAMSON, ALEXANDER, born 1845, son of the late

George Williamson in Kirkcaldy, Fife, died in Hamburg on 1 May 1878. [Fife Herald]

WILLIAMSON, JOHN, from the Diocese of Aberdeen, matriculated at the University of Koln in 1498. [SNQ.X.3/78]

WILSON, GEORGE, born in Aberdeen on 15 November 1832, was at the Ratisbon Seminary in 1852, ordained as a priest and returned to Scotland. [SIG#296][RSC#I.258]

WILSON, JOHN, possibly from Culross, an officer in the service of the Prince of Luneburg at Winsen, 1672. [NRS.GD29/2152]

WILSON, MAGNUS, a shipmaster in Bremen, master of the Countess of Kincardine, 1676. [NRS.AC7.4]

WINGATE, ..., son of Reverend William Wingate, was born in Pest, Hungary, on 6 July 1846. [W#VII.699]

WINGRAVE, MATTHEW, of Kirkbank Villa, Morningside, Edinburgh, died in Bonn on 23 November 1848, inventory, 1851, Comm. Edinburgh. [NRS]

WINGRAVE, WILLIAM MEARNS, in Bonn, Germany, 11 April 1850, son of Matthew Wingrave in Kirkbank, Edinburgh who died on 23 November 1848. [NRS.B22.4.60.34][NRS.S/H]

WISEMAN, JOHN, born in Buckie, Banffshire, on 5 July 1833, was at the Ratisbon Seminary from 1845 to 1850, died in Leith during 1875. [SIG#296] [RSC#I.257]

WONDERLY, JOHN N., born in Germany during 1836, a watchmaker and jeweller residing in the Govan Poorhouse in 1881. [1881 Census]

WOOD, WILLIAM, a student at the University of Heidelberg, 1570. [SIG#314][SHR.V/67]

WORDIEMAN, HERMAN, a merchant of Bremen, then in
Leith, 1712. [NRS.AC8.152]

WREDE, LUCAS, master of the St Lucas of Hamburg, 1627.
[NRS.AC7.1.35]

WREY, GEORGE, in Germany, 1873. [NRS.GD21/479]

WRIGHT, JAMES, ("Jacobus Faber"), a student at the
University of Rostock in 1593. [SIG#313]

WRIGHT, JOHN, son of John Wright and his wife Marjory
Paterson in Newton of Balquhan, died in Prussia during
February 1595. [APB]

WRIGHT, RICHARD NORTON, married Williamina
Ballentine, youngest daughter of the late Alexander
Ballentine in Edinburgh, at the British Embassy in Dresden
on 3 January 1857. [W.XVIII.1834]

WYLLY, DAVID, a merchant in Hamburg, was admitted as a
burgess of Montrose, Angus, in 1773. [Montrose Burgess
Roll]; his sister Elizabeth Wyllie at Hillend of Woodston,
testament, 1792, Comm. St Andrews. [NRS]

YOUNG, ALEXANDER, was at Ratisbon Seminary in 1772.
[SIG#295][RSC#I.253]

YOUNG, ANDREW, a merchant in Hamburg, died in Edinburgh,
5 July 1853, inventory, 1861, Comm. Edinburgh. [NRS]

YOUNG, DAVID, educated at the Braunsberg Seminary around
1580. [SIG#298]

YOUNG, RICHARD, married Catherine Shipham, in Hamburg,
1634. [TKH]

YOUNG, THOMAS, son of William Young a minister in
Perthshire, educated at St Andrews University around 1606,
minister to the Merchant Adventurers in Hamburg during

1620s.

YOUNG, WILLIAM, a Major in the service of the Prince of
Brunswick, 1764. [NRS.RS23.XIX.504]; served heir to his
uncle William Wallace of Carzield, 1766. [NRS.Retours]

YULL, GEORGE T., son of Mr Yull in Little Ardo,
Aberdeenshire, married Hermin, eldest daughter of George
Kosma of Neutra, Hungary, there on 19 January 1862.
[AJ#5955]

ZEBBES, ZACHARIAS, born in Rostock around 1643, a sugar-
boiler in Rotterdam, later at the Easter Sugary in Glasgow,
1669, died in Glasgow in December 1679.
[GA][NNQ.1.13][NRS.Russell mss]

ZIEGLER, ALEXANDER, son of George Ziegler, a glover at
the Windmill, was apprenticed to Alexander Campbell, a
goldsmith in Edinburgh, on 2 December 1747; a deed, 31
August 1781. [ERA][NRS.RD4.230.428]

ZIEGLER, GEORGE, a goldsmith in Canongate, Edinburgh,
around 1690-1702. [NRS.RD2.86.2.141]

ZIEGLER, JOHN, a cloth merchant in Leith, 1820s.
[NRS.CS236/Sed.Bk.2/1]

ZIEGLAR, MICHAEL, a jeweller in Canongate, Edinburgh,
1683, his widow Amphillus, 1700.
[OEC.19.19][NRS.RD4.87.521]

ZIEGLER, WILLIAM, from Scotland, a medical graduate of
Edinburgh University, 1849. [EMG#165]

SOME SHIPPING LINKS

Alexander and James of Anstruther, master James Beat, arrived in Anstruther from Hamburg, 1755. [NRS.E504.3.3]

Angel of Grippiswald, master Patrick Storving, arrived in Dundee from Grippiswald, 2 May 1614. [DSL][SIG#25]

Ann of Leith, master Samuel Pew, from Anstruther to Hamburg, 1763. [NRS.E504.3.4]

Ann and Catherine of Leith, master James Redlay, from Anstruther to Hamburg, 1744. [NRS.E504.3.1]

Anna of Flekkefjord, master Anders Larsen, trading between Montrose, Hamburg, and Lubeck, in 1750. [NRS.E504.24.1]

Anna Margreta, master Johan Delejen, from Greenock to Bremen in May 1760. [NRS.E504.15.9]

Anne of Leith, master Thomas Masterman, trading between Leith and Bremen, in 1747. [NRS.AC8.691]

Archangel of Leith, master William Robertson, from Aberdeen *with 300 soldiers* bound for the port of Gluckstadt in Germany, 1612. [NRS.GD84.Sec.2/154]

Bamburgh Fisher, master James Pollock, from Anstruther to Hamburg, 1753. [NRS.E504.3.2]

Barbara of Dundee, master David Simpson, trading between Dundee and Bremen. 1750. [NRS.E504.11.2]

Blessing of Aberdeen, master John Gordon, trading between Aberdeen and Hamburg, 1744. [NRS.E504.1.1]

Brenilid of Hamburg, master Henry Mayer, trading between Leith and Hamburg, 1667. [NRS.E72.15.6]

Buxton of Dundee, master Robert Ross, trading between Dundee and Bremen 1749. [NRS.E504.11.2]

Caroline of Newcastle, a brigantine, master William Wilkinson , from Hamburgh to Dundee in 1801. [NRS.CE70.1.9]

Catherina of Hamburg, master Peter Laders, from Kirkcaldy to Hamburg in May 1754. [NRS.E504.20.3]

Charles of Dundee, master Robert Bennet, trading between Dundee and Bremen, 1728. [NRS.CE70]

Charming Peggy of Montrose, master Robert Mudie, trading between Montrose and Hamburg, 1743-1744. [NRS.E504.24.1]

Codfisher of Aberdeen, master Benjamin Ballantyne, trading

between Aberdeen and Hamburg, 1743. [NRS.E504.1.1]

Concordia of Bremen, master Albert Hillars, trading between
Altona and Lerwick, 1744. [NRS.E504.32/1]

Culloden of Newcastle, master Patrick Forsyth, trading between
Aberdeen and Hamburg, 1748. [NRS.E504.1.2]

Dow, trading between Stralsund and Dundee, 1612. [SIG#25]

Earl of Dumfries of Dundee, master Robert Leslie, trading
between Perth and Hamburg, 1762. [NRS.E504.27]

Eleanor of Leith, trading between the Shetland Islands and
Hamburg, 1749. [NRS.AC10.342]

Elizabeth and Anne, master James Brown, trading between
Dundee and Hamburg, 1747. [NRS.E504.11.2]

Endeavour of Montrose, master John Dunbar, trading between
Montrose and Hamburg, 1749-1750. [NRS.E504.24.2]

Fisher of Leith, master John Craig, trading between Perth and
Hamburg, 1727. [NRS.CE52]

Fortune, trading between Emden and Dundee, 1603. [SIG#28]

Friendship of Nordeney, from Hamburg to Dundee in May 1801.
[NRS.CE70.1.9]

Grace of God, trading between Dundee and Lubeck, 1583.
[SIG#25]

Frommagicht of Altona, master Petter Andersen, trading between
Lerwick and Hamburg, 1744. [NRS.E504.33/1]

Happy Janet of Leith, master ....Dick, trading between Leith and
Bremen, 1752. [AJ#241]

Helleanor of Holy Island, master John Taylor, trading between
Aberdeen and Hamburg, 1749. [NRS.E504.1.3]

Hettle Blott of Keil, master Mieneret Wienertz, trading between
Lerwick and Hamburg, 1746. [NRS.E504.32/1]

Hope of Wismar, master Joachim Wittenburg, trading between
Lubeck and Leith, 1672. [NRS.E72.15.12]

Hope of Hamburg, master Nicolas Rickman, trading between
Leith and Hamburg, 1673. [NRS.E72.15.14/17]

Hope of Leith, master John Williamson, from Kirkcaldy to
Hamburg in May 1754. [NRS.E504.20.3]

Industry, master John Finlay, from Leith to Hamburg in August
1769. [NRS.E504.22.15]

James and Jane of Montrose, master James Dickie, from
Anstruther to Hamburg, 1762. [NRS.E504.3.3]

James and Margaret of Montrose, master James Henderson,

trading between Montrose, Hamburg, and Bremen, 1743-
1750. [NRS.E504.24.2]

James and Margaret, arrived in Dundee from Emden, 1775.
[NRS.E504.11.9]

James and Peggy of Montrose, master James Mudie, trading
between Montrose and Hamburg, 1746-1750.
[NRS.E504.24.1/2]

Janet of Elie, master James Young, from Elie to Bremen, 1711.
[NRS.AC8.127]

Jeannie of Greenock, master Robert Eason, from Greenock to Bremen,
1769. [NRS.E504.15.17]

John, master Johan Frederick Daanikan, from Greenock to
Bremen in May 1760. [NRS.E504.115.9]

JoNRS of Dundee, master George Knight, arrived Dundee from
Lubeck, 1616. [DSL][SIG#26]

Kroon, master Peter Claasen, from Greenock to Hamburg in May
1760. [NRS.E504.15.9]

Lady Lucretia, master Laurence Birk, from Greenock to Hamburg
in June 1760. [NRS.E504.15.9]

Leathly of Aberdeen, master John Lickly, trading between
Aberdeen and Hamburg, 1750. [NRS.E504.1.3]

Little Pink, trading between Dundee and Lubeck, 1582. [SIG#25]

Margaret of Inverness, master George Roger, trading between
Inverness and Hamburg in 1716. [SIL#25]

Margaret of Fraserburgh, master John Noble, from Hamburg to
Scotland, 1728. [NRS.AC8.379]

Margaret of Arbroath, master William Kenny, trading between
Montrose and Hamburg, 1750. [NRS.E504.24.2]

Margaret and Ann of Aberdeen, master George Shepherd, trading
between Montrose and Hamburg, 1745. [NRS.E504.24.1]

Maaria Catherina of Oldenburg, from Bremen to Dundee in April
1801. [NRS.CE70.1.9]

Marjory and Anne of Montrose, master William Napier, trading
between Aberdeen and Hamburg, 1749. [NRS.E504.1.3]

Mary of Perth, master James Sime, from Bremen to Dundee, July
1790. [NRS.CE70.1.7]

Mary and Jean of Aberdeen, master Charles More, trading
between Montrose and Hamburg, 1745. [NRS.E504.24.1]

Mary and Jean of Airth, master John McKie, trading between
Aberdeen and Hamburg, 1750. [NRS.E504.1.3]

Merry Plowman, master James Smith, trading between Dundee
and Hamburg, 1755. [NRS.E504.11.3]

Morning Star of Papingberg, to Dundee in 1801. [NRS.CE70.1.9]

Neptune, trading between Emden and Dundee, 1603. [SIG#28]

Rabuck of Stralsund, master David Nisiep, arrived in Dundee from
Stralsund, 15 April 1617. [DSL]

Providence of Aberdeen, master George Buchan trading between
Aberdeen and Hamburg, 1751. [NRS.E504.1.3]

Richardson and Sandeman of Perth, master John Petrie, trading
between Perth and Hamburg, 1765. [NRS.E504.27]

Roebuck, trading between Stralsund and Dundee, 1617. [SIG#26]

Roland of Bremen, master John Harmonson, trading between
Leith and Hamburg, 1672-1673. [NRS.E72.15.14]

St John of Hamburg, master Claus Petersen, trading between Leith
and Hamburg, 1681. [NRS.E72.15.21]

St Marie of Lubeck, master Henrick Schultz, wrecked near
Peterhead in 1628. [RPCS.II.274]

St Peter of Altona, master Henrick Van Duven, trading between
Lerwick and Hamburg, 1747. [NRS.E504.32/1]

Seaflower of Arbroath, master John Low, trading between
Montrose and Hamburg, 1748. [NRS.E504.24.2]

Serpent's Prize of Leith, master James Stephen, trading between
Perth and Hamburg, 1748. [NRS.E504.27]

Sibella of Lerwick, master William Farquhar, trading between the
Shetland Islands and Hamburg from 1743 to 1753.
[NRS.GD144][NRS.E504.32/1]

Simon of Hamburg, master Richard Richardson, arrived in Leith
on 2 June 1666 from Hamburg. [NRS.E72.15.2]

Springhart of Bremen, master Herman Viollisen, trading between
Leith and Bremen, 1680. [NRS.E72.15.21]

Success of Inverness, master Alexander Dunbar, trading between
Inverness and Hamburg in 1716. [SIL#25]

Thomas and Betty of Montrose, master David English, trading
between Montrose and Hamburg, 1749-1750; master Robert
Mudie, trading between Aberdeen and Hamburg, 1750.
[NRS.E504.24/2; E504.1.3]

Two Brothers of Emden, from Hamburg to Dundee in May 1801.
[NRS.CE70.1.9]

Two White Falcons of Hamburg, master Gerrard Hermon, from
Hamburg to Leith in March 1650. [Edinburgh Burgh

Records]
Vrow Girthut, from Hamburg to Dundee in May 1801.
[NRS.CE70.1.9]
Vrow Helena of Stadt, from Hamburg to Dundee in May 1801.
[NRS.CE70.1.9]
William and James of Prestonpans, master John Gillies,from
Inverness to Hamburg, 1717. [SIL#36]
York of New York, a snow, master Joseph Wilson, trading
between Lerwick, Shetland Islands, and Hamburg, in 1747.
[NRS.E504.31.1]

REFERENCES

ABR =   Ayr Burgess Roll

ACA =   Aberdeen City Archives

AJ   =   Aberdeen Journal, series

CBR =   Register of the Burgesses of the Burgh of the
            Canongate, H. Armet, [Edinburgh, 1951]

DA   =   Dundee Advertiser, series

DAC   =   Danish Archives, Copenhagen

DPCA =   Dundee, Perth and Cupar Advertiser, series

DSL   =   Dundee Shipping Lists

EBR   =   Roll of Edinburgh Burgesses and Guildbrethren,
            1701-1760, C.Boog-Watson, [Edinburgh, 1929]

EC   =   Edinburgh Courant, series

EEC   =   Edinburgh Evening Courant, series

ECA   =   Edinburgh City Archives

EEC =　　　Edinburgh Evening Courant, series

EFR =　　　East Fife Reporter, series

EMG =　　　List of the Graduates in Medicine in the
　　　　　　University of Edinburgh from 1705-1867.
　　　　　　[Edinburgh, 1867]

EUL =　　　Edinburgh University Library

F　　=　　　Fasti Ecclesiae Scoticanae, H. Scott,
　　　　　　[Edinburgh, 1917]

GA　=　　　Greenock Advertiser, series

GBR =　　　Burgesses & Guild Brethren of Glasgow, 1573-
　　　　　　1750, J. R. Anderson, [Edinburgh, 1925]

GH　=　　　Glasgow Herald, series

GM　=　　　Gentleman's Magazine, series
HG　=　　　House of Gordon, Volume III, [Aberdeen, 1907]

HKA =　　　Heimatkalendar fur den Kreis Anklam,
　　　　　　M. Bethe, [Anklam, 1931]

HL　=　　　Hay of Leyes Papers, ms

HMC =　　　Historic Manuscripts Commission, series

IR　=　　　Innes Review, series

JTA =　　　Journals of Sir Thomas Allen, R. C. Anderson,
　　　　　　[London, 1993]

KCA =　　　Officers and Graduates of King's College Aberdeen,
　　　　　　J. Anderson, [Aberdeen, 1863]

MAM=　　　Memoirs of Andrew Melville, [London, 1918]

MBR =   Montrose Burgess Roll

MGIF=   Military Governors and Imperial Frontiers,
         A. Mackillop and S. Murdoch, [Leiden, 2003]

MSC =   Miscellany of the Spalding Society, series

NA   =   National Archives, London

NRS =   National Archives of Scotland, Edinburgh

NNQ =   Northern Notes and Queries, series

OEC =   Book of the Old Edinburgh Club, series

PCC =   Prerogative Court of Canterbury, London

PJ   =   People's Journal, series

RGG =   Roll of Graduates of the University of Glasgow,
         1712-1897, W. I. Anderson, [Glasgow, 1898]

RGS =   Register of the Great Seal of Scotland, series

RHCA =   Regimental History of the Covenanting Armies,
         1639-1651, E. Furgol, [Edinburgh, 1990]

RPCS=   Register of the Privy Council of Scotland, series

RSC =   Records of the Scots Colleges, [Aberdeen, 1906]

S   =   Scotsman, series, Edinburgh

SAH =   Staats Archiv, Hamburg

SAUR=   Biographical Register of the University of St
         Andrews 1747-1897, R N Smart, [St Andrews,
         2004]

SD   =   Shetland Documents, [Edinburgh, 1994/1999]

SGen =   The Scottish Genealogist, series

SF   =   The Scots in Franconia, M. Dilworth,
             [Edinburgh, 1974]

SIG   =   The Scots in Germany, T.A.Fischer,
             [Edinburgh, 1902]

SIL   =   Letterbook of bailie John Stewart of
             Inverness, [Edinburgh, 1915]

SLIR =   Irregular Marriages in the South Leith
             Kirk Session Records, 1697-1818.
             [Edinburgh, 1968]

SNQ   =   Scottish Notes and Queries, series

SP   =   The Scots Peerage, Sir J.B.Paul, [Edinburgh, 1909]

SSNE =   Scotland, Scandinavia and Northern Europe
             Database, 1580-1707

STAUL   St Andrews University Library

STW =   Scotland and the Thirty Years War 1618-1648,
             S. Murdoch, [Leiden, 2001]

TKH   =   Trauregister aus den altesten Kirchenbuchern
             Hamburgs

VDHS =   Verzeichnis der Hamburger Shetland Fahrer,
             1547-1646, P.Pipen, [Hamburg, 1988]

W   =   Witness, series

WMF =   Calendar of Writs of Monro of Fowlis, 1299-1823,
             C. T. Macinnes, [Edinburgh, 1940]

www.ingramcontent.com/pod-product-compliance
Lightning Source LLC
Chambersburg PA
CBHW070925270326
41927CB00011B/2723